PRAISE FOR *THE ICONIST*

"Human attention span is today's and forever's scarcity. Jamie Mustard saw the trend early. He studied and lived it deeply. He cracked the code. *The Iconist* is a must-read for all entrepreneurs, venture capitalists, CEOs, and shapers of opinion."

—Rich Karlgaard, publisher, *Forbes*

"We all have a yearning to matter to the world. Jamie Mustard has provided a road map for each of us to be heard and leave a legacy in the noise of our new digital lives. This sparkling and practical book is alive with fresh ideas."

—Daniel Pink, author, *When*, *Drive*, and *A Whole New Mind*

"In a marketplace that's more crowded, noisy, and confusing than ever, it's harder than ever to stand out and be noticed—whether you're designing a product, selling a service, or marketing yourself. Jamie Mustard offers a remarkable set of provocative ideas and a collection of engaging case studies to meet the defining business challenge of our time. *The Iconist* is itself a standout, as useful as it is original."

—William C. Taylor, cofounder and founding editor, *Fast Company* and author, *Simply Brilliant*

"The design world has always known the power of icons, but until now had little idea of how to get there. Mustard explains all in his brilliant book."

—Clive Wilkinson, workplace design pioneer, Googleplex architect, and listed in *Fast Company*'s 100 Most Creative People and Master of Design

"In order to get innovations into the world we first have to figure out how to get them seen and heard. *The Iconist* has amazingly codified a set of laws that will get anyone to take a close look at any creation."

—**Carl Arnese, senior design director, FUTURE innovation, Adidas**

"Jamie Mustard's secret to standing out is steeped in creativity and common sense. In *The Iconist*, he offers his fresh yet timeless perspective on how to break through the clutter and get yourself, your product, and your message noticed. An easy, insightful read."

—**Joanne Gordon, coauthor, *Onward: How Starbucks Fought for Its Life without Losing Its Soul***

"In my thirty years of representing speakers, leaders, and thinkers including Jimmy Carter, Carl Sagan, Desmond Tutu, Peter Drucker, Jared Diamond, Margaret Atwood, Malcolm Gladwell, and Hunter S Thompson, to name a few, I have seen, studied, and lived with a lot of ideas. I can say from this unique vantage point that *The Iconist* is special. Imagine that you are driving on a winding mountain road as dusk approaches. As it gets darker you turn on your lights. Fog emerges and becomes thicker as time goes on. The once helpful car lights are now blinding in the fog. You must slow down, and eventually, you decide to pull over when the fog becomes too thick and too hard to get through. Now think of the fog as the information that bombards us every day. The very tools and skills used to navigate the road ahead become a hindrance when the fog grows thick. *The Iconist* provides you with a new tool kit and expertise to pierce through the fog. In a world where each of us is struggling to matter, Jamie Mustard provides us hope for the future."

—**Michael Humphrey, CEO, NextUp Speakers**

"Jamie Mustard's gripping insights into the economics of attention offer real solutions for building connection. Amidst a proliferation of choices, Mustard shares foolproof systems for getting seen, heard, and remembered."

—Kimberly Barta, former global brand leader, Dr.
Martens, Sorel, and CMO, Nike Valiant Labs

"Jamie Mustard's *The Iconist* answers a core question on building great customer relationships: How do we capture their attention and make us forever memorable in their life? This is truly an important book."

—Jeanne Bliss, former chief customer officer, Microsoft,
and author, *Chief Customer Officer*, *Would You Do That to
Your Mother*, and *I Love You More Than My Dog*

"A great book for people who want to truly know how to be seen."

—Don Tuski, president, College for Creative Studies

"A powerful book filled with profound and pragmatic insights. Mustard single-handedly shatters the mystique surrounding successful branding and disruption. A must-read for those who aspire to be on the vanguard of change."

—Rebecca D. Costa, sociobiologist, futurist,
and author, *The Watchman's Rattle*

"If you want to be heard in today's noisy world, shut up and read this book."

—Jim Riswold, author, *Hitler Saved My Life*

"As a media professional where getting attention and grabbing eyeballs is everything, I found this book an essential read and a deeply valuable guide for commanding attention in today's high-speed world."

—Bobby Souers, media director, Wieden+Kennedy

"Jamie has pinpointed what makes one song a hit—and another, a dud. And Blocks work beyond song creation, but to how radio programmers should approach building their radio station."

—Cort Johnson, program director, 101.9 KINK FM, Alpha Broadcasting

"I already feel smarter talking to my colleagues just having read this book. Jamie has tapped into something primal here. *The Iconist* has literally transformed the way I look at product development. I will never look at a single product or product line the same way again."

—Hans Albing, product manager, Under Armour

"The tricky thing about simplicity is it's hard. Making anything seem easy takes a lot of careful work. Connecting dots across music, cultures, genres, disciplines, decades, and centuries, Jamie Mustard shows us the strength of simplicity—how it inspires, endures, and can be applied every day. He makes it look easy, too.

—Ryan White, author, *Springsteen: Album by Album*
and *Jimmy Buffett: A Good Life All the Way*

"*The Iconist* should be required reading for anyone endeavoring to communicate a message (hell, even just survive) within the maelstrom of today's information overload. Jamie's approach will redefine how you think."

—Derek Welch, cofounder, Big-Giant, UNKL

"*The Iconist* captures the duality of life in our overloaded technological world . . . on the one hand we have greater access to more information than ever before, and on the other we experience more anxiety, depression, and hopelessness about how to digest the plethora of data for our own lives. With *The Iconist* we have a clear road map to find sanity and success in our hyperspeed world. A must-read for anyone puzzled by what life's going to be like tomorrow. *The Iconist* is a true original."

—Michael Morrow, founder, Nutcase Helmets

"*The Iconist* compels questions of great urgency and relevance to the health of the social matrix that gives our lives meaning and purpose. It is excellent."

—Shauna H Springer, PhD, world's leading authority on PTSD and moral injuries, and senior director, TAPS Red Team

"This book has set forth a method to allow any complex science and engineering to be understood and appreciated by all. If you are trying to make a complicated thing simple, understood, and desired, in a world full of noise, *The Iconist* is the solution."

—Tibi Iovu, mission control ace, Cassini Spacecraft, JPL/NASA

THE
ICONIST

THE
ICONIST

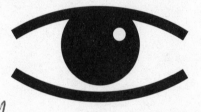

THE ART AND SCIENCE
OF STANDING OUT
JAMIE MUSTARD

BenBella

BenBella Books, Inc.
Dallas, TX

BenBella

BenBella Books, Inc.
10440 N. Central Expressway, Suite 800
Dallas, TX 75231
www.benbellabooks.com
Send feedback to feedback@benbellabooks.com

Printed in the United States of America
10 9 8 7 6 5 4 3 2 1

Library of Congress Cataloging-in-Publication Control Number: 2019015073
ISBN 9781948836418 (paper over board)
ISBN 9781948836661 (electronic)

Editing by Claire Schulz
Copyediting by Miki Alexandra Caputo
Proofreading by Lisa Story and Laura Cherkas
Indexing by WordCo Indexing Services, Inc.
Text design and composition by Aaron Edmiston
Cover design and illustration by Mark Slotemaker
Interior illustrations by Mark Slotemaker (additional photo credits on page 241)
Printed by Lake Book Manufacturing

Distributed to the trade by Two Rivers Distribution, an Ingram brand
www.tworiversdistribution.com

With much appreciation

My profound thanks to my good friend and indispensable collaborator, H. Shaw Thomas, without whose unwavering passion, dedication, hard work, and editorial contribution this project could not have been completed.

Shaw, this book belongs to the both of us.

My deepest gratitude to Chris Young, editor in chief of Vortex Music Magazine, *for getting me started on this journey. His research, advice, work, and continued support have been invaluable.*

For my nine-year-old self and the angels
that helped him along his way

CONTENTS

PART THREE

PART FOUR

INTRODUCTION

If we do not grab the attention of others immediately, we could lose them forever.
There is no doubt that technology has made our lives eas-
ier, but it has also made our lives harder in invisible ways.
Technology-induced change has created an explosion of content and choice—a deluge of products, services, and voices
in constant competition for our attention. In our always-on,
internet-connected world, wave after wave of information bombards our senses and dilutes our individual voices. Whether
we are conscious of it or not, we're drowning in a sea of white
noise.

As noise around us grows into a never-ending thrum, it
reduces our ability to hear one another. Artists struggle to grow
their audiences. Writers fail to retain readers' concentration.
Advertisers' work fails to generate sales. Innovators can't get
support for their ideas. Businesses have a harder time attracting new customers. We're trying to stand out but because of the
digital onslaught, people are so overwhelmed that they are only
partially paying attention.

Being noticed is the first step to success. Being remembered
is the next. But those two factors have become nearly impossible
to control. How can you guarantee that anyone will look at what
you're doing in a sea of other options? How can you be sure you'll
stick in their minds?

The Iconist solves this problem.

Taking lessons from history, psychology, the arts, and pop culture, *The Iconist* provides a clear formula to help you stand out, be heard, and be *remembered* at will. At the start of any connection we need to speak simply to be understood. *The Iconist* gives you an easy-to-use manual on how to distill yourself down, no matter what you do, and lead with the right simple message to grab attention from others. This book is a handbook to achieve **radical simplicity**. And these days, it is *only* simplicity that gets attention.

I currently work as a messaging, design, and communications expert, consulting with entrepreneurs and new businesses as well as successful artists, brands, CEOs, and innovators (some of whose stories are in this book). All of them, even the highly successful ones, came to me struggling to be heard in a world overloaded with too much of everything.

My unconventional life's journey led me to explore the art and science of standing out, and eventually uncover a solution that can help everyone. As a child of poverty and neglect I was rarely in school and had little parental supervision. It was a confusing time for me; my days were shapeless and my focus was scattered. As a kid, time already seemed to move slowly; the smog-refracted sun of the polluted Los Angeles sky only added to my languor. Burning gray concrete was the only world I knew; I recall struggling to remember what rain looked like.

In these barren L.A. neighborhoods, we were the featureless, future-less kids that would eventually serve as America's lower rung. I feared my future would be an agonizing one of physical labor and drudgery. Eventually, I turned things around, graduating high school and then going on to attend the London School of Economics. Yet it would be twenty years before I realized that the seeds sown in those early years of deprivation, invisibility, and struggle were the precursors to a major passion in my adult life: discovering what it takes to make something—anything— STAND OUT despite the avalanche of information in the world. My work has focused essentially on the "economics of attention."

The reason we pay attention and remember something is based in our innate perceptions and a set of unchanging primal laws that I call Blocks. Blocks are the simple mechanism underlying what makes anything iconic. In some form or another, Blocks have always existed in the world. A Block is the primal elementary form, sound, or phrase that, once repeated, makes anything iconic, able to break through and stick in any onlooker's mind. Through instant recognizability and repetition, a Block becomes an Icon in the mind.

The beginnings of the idea underlying Blocks took root in my mind while I was studying the work of the architect Louis Kahn. Kahn was the subject of a 2003 Academy Award–nominated documentary directed by his son, Nathaniel. Kahn became what many experts consider to be the most significant architect of the twentieth century—but only in the waning years of his life.

As I sat in a tiny independent film theater, watching the documentary on Kahn's architecture, something about the unforgettable, bold, monolithic nature of his work triggered a memory of a Billy Joel interview I had read as a teenager. Joel was asked why he was able to write *so many* hits. Joel said that he was more interested in *what made music last* than what made it beautiful, fun, or artistic. He said in his youth he worked hard to be more of a musicologist than a musician. Most of all he wanted to know *why* Beethoven's Fifth (you know, *dun–dun–da-dun!*) had remained relevant for over two centuries. I had spent almost fifteen years pondering this question.

So, as I sat learning about the work of a very different creator, I started wondering if there was a connection between Kahn's monolithic structures and Joel's repetitive melodies. It was as though a spark went off—my skin actually got hot.

With my background in economic history, I set out to see if there were in fact patterns of iconic communication. Was there an economics of attention? What makes some things imprint in the mind while other things are repelled? What causes any business, science, art, idea, or message to stand out and become iconic?

How would this function at a time when it has become damn near impossible to be seen among such an overwhelming amount of messaging, products, and services in the world?

What I found turned my head around, having implications far beyond music and buildings.

I spent the next decade testing and trying to consolidate and codify a set of rules for what I found. In the end, they were actually very simple. So simple that even though examples exist everywhere, all around us, we don't often notice them. I consulted some of the leading tech innovators, social change agents, CEOs, trailblazing engineers, designers, artists, and rock stars in the world about what causes something to stand out and take hold in the mind. It turns out the principles work across any medium—from music to visual art, design, public speaking, even drafting an email, résumé, or dating profile. Anyone can use the principles of human perception in this book to get attention for the things they care about. These principles—I think of them as timeless primordial laws—are the foundation of my work with businesses and individuals today.

Now, there have been many books written on the subject of why something stands out, sticks, and endures; however, many of them fall short because they are trying to grasp a very simple mechanism but end up overcomplicating it. They don't clearly articulate the primordial rules of *why* people pay attention, and in turn, that makes it hard for you to use the actual rules that do exist.

What makes some things imprint in the mind while other things are repelled? What causes any business, science, art, idea, or message to stand out and become iconic?

In *The Iconist*, I will teach you how to stand out, capture attention, and imprint in the mind. Whatever field you work in, I will show you how to use these patterns of human perception to craft completely irresistible content that demands engagement from others. Despite its simplicity, what makes something catch our eye is so obvious that it can be hard to see. So much of the time we're so close to our art or work that we can't understand how to value it and represent ourselves with simplicity to grab the attention we deserve. I am offering you a formula to get this right every time. The stories I'll tell here show the irresistible laws of attention from many angles so that everyone from a child to a CEO can use them.

Within this book you are going to meet many of the business leaders, scientists, artists, designers, historical figures, and social change and culture makers who inspire me and whose work gets me out of bed in the morning. I have been fortunate enough to know many of the people you will read about and feel grateful to call many of them friends.

In my journey from extreme illiteracy and poverty to the London School of Economics and relative prosperity, I've observed that no matter our life circumstances, many of us feel the weight of obscurity, at least in relation to our personal dreams. Fear of failure is what most often keeps us from going after what we want. The mechanism of how Blocks and Icons work is as simple as a lever and I hope you use it to reach your greatest dreams and aspirations.

—Jamie

WHEN READING THIS BOOK

The Iconist paints a picture of the world we live in and explains what will *actually* stand out in that world, no matter the level of distraction and competition for attention. It then gives you the formula and direction to produce your own Icons. Because the same rules apply across all media and content categories, it's not as simple as giving you a template or paint-by-number directives, but by teaching you to think like an "Iconist," I hope to show you how to think about and present your work in a totally new (and deeply affecting) way.

The Problem: The first part of the book lays out the scope of the problem—what our constantly connected world means for everyday people in terms of our focus and personal outlook, and the problems it poses for anyone trying to reach an audience.

Standing Out—BASED ON PRIMAL LAWS: The second part dives deeper into Blocks and Icons—the psychology that explains their deceptively simple power—and offers clear examples so that you'll immediately begin to recognize Blocks and Icons when you see them "in the wild."

How You Can Use These Laws in Your Personal Endeavors: The third part lays out basic principles for using Blocks no matter what work you do so that you can use the laws of attention to be heard, seen, and remembered in any professional or creative pursuit.

How to Use Transparency to Speed Up the Process: Last, the fourth part of the book addresses transparency in terms of how we all connect in a digital world. Traditional selling is out; being authentic with transparent, digestible facts and real content is all that is credible today. The digital world has completely transformed how we connect to and perceive the world around us.

When you understand these pillars you really can get the attention you want, at will.

WHAT IS AN ICONIST?

1

Boldness be my friend!
—**William Shakespeare**, *Cymbeline*

Imagine you are in a museum of ancient art filled with thousands upon thousands of old and beautiful paintings and you stop to look at one. Many of us think the reason we stop at one particular painting is random, but it is not.

The same is true for music. Say one evening you decide to walk down the Sunset Strip in Los Angeles and pass by every venue on the club-packed entertainment street in the heart of the city, between Crescent Heights and Doheny—the gateway between West Hollywood and Beverly Hills. If one band's sound made you stop, stay, and listen, there would actually be a reason—and it would have nothing to do with your musical taste.

You would almost certainly be unaware of the reason other than you "liked it" or it was "your kind of music," but the real reason is much more primal. And once you understand the laws of attention and attraction, you will not only see these laws working everywhere and all around you but can use them to get attention for anything you choose.

Despite the intense distractions of the modern world, certain ideas, art, advertising, scientific theory, and messages *do* stand out, while others are ignored. The reason we pay attention to certain people and ignore others isn't necessarily because their work is fresher, more beautiful, or more innovative than someone else's (though it may be).

The real reason is rooted in primal laws of human perception—how people take in and filter information. An "Iconist" is someone who has mastered these laws, and gets others to pay attention. He or she knows how people prefer to take in information . . . and what makes them filter it out.

Iconists use massively oversized, bold images or phrases that can be instantly understood. They do this by counterintuitively using repetition to grab attention. While we're often taught that repeating ourselves is not effective, it actually allows Iconists to generate increased interest and support for their message. It sounds simple. But few of us know how to use these iconic techniques, even though they can help us earn more of the things we want in nearly every area of our lives.

The Iconist centers around the concept of Icons and Blocks, which are similar ideas, but with a key distinction. A Block is a succinct, clear, bold, monolithic image, statement, melody, physical structure, or piece of design. Throughout the book we'll explore examples, but what makes a Block a Block is that it can be immediately understood by any onlooker. By definition, a Block has not yet taken hold in the mind of the viewer or audience. It is an Icon in the making or an Icon about to happen. With consistent, deliberate, and up-front repetition, the Block grabs attention, stands out, and imprints itself in the minds of those you are trying to reach. In fact, if done correctly, it gives your intended audience no choice. That is when your Block becomes an Icon—once it has been accepted and imprinted in the minds of others.

When I use the capitalized word *Icon* in this book, I am referring to an Icon that has been made with a Block. Since these two terms are so closely related, it is not uncommon for my clients to refer to using Blocks as "Iconing" something, or to say, "I Icon'd it!"

Blocks, as tools to create Icons, work in all mediums and can be used with anything from art, music, design, or architecture to business and product design. In other words you can make anything stand out in any medium once you understand these timeless rules of human perception.

We often have no idea how simple a concept needs to be to stand out and how much repetition it takes for a message to demand attention, sink in, and then endure with our desired audience. People tend to think that once we have said it once, the message has been received and there's no need to draw more attention to it. This is because most people are, for reasons we will explore, uncomfortable truly standing out and being consistently obvious. It can be a catch-22—we want to stand out and get others to champion our work, but it can also be awkward to have all eyes upon us. A true Iconist pushes past this discomfort.

Distilling a message down to its most simplistic, elementary ideal can be difficult because people are complicated. Our thoughts and emotions combine in ways that make it hard to break down what we want to say into a few obvious points. Yet human beings can best digest information when it's presented in a few simple points that they can latch on to in an instant, no matter how complex the idea or product may be.

When we lead with *radical simplicity* everything changes. We *make* connection happen purposefully through deliberately crafted approaches that gain immediate attention, rather than by chance. By following the examples in this book, you'll learn to transform yourself into an iconic thinker, and you'll likely become more fulfilled personally as a result.

There may be moments you are using the laws laid out in *The Iconist* when you will be tempted to make your message more complicated than it needs to be. Don't give in. We often feel uncomfortable being bold, but we're also much happier people when we embrace fierce simplicity. It is instant understandability and instant comprehension that facilitate connection.

As an Iconist you can communicate in such a way that your recipients will not be able to get your message out of their heads, regardless of how you currently see yourself as a communicator. Any art, political message, film, advertising, music, writing, innovation, or profession can rise above the competing environment and demand attention if you use the natural laws of Blocks and Icons.

Don't forget: the ability to express yourself and the ability to be heard are two very different things. We can express and fall on deaf ears. To get what we want, others must be listening. And as we will see, breaking through all the noise so that others can hear, without using Blocks, has become nearly impossible.

PART ONE

FRESH AIR

2

Meaning and reality were not hidden somewhere
behind things, they were in them, in all of them.
—Hermann Hesse, *Siddhartha*

In the mid-2000s a courageous South American city government rejected media
and messaging overload on an unlikely and almost unbelievable
scale. In the process, it revealed the hidden life of one of the
world's most vibrant cities. This bold, revolutionary policy was
enacted by the municipal government of São Paulo, Brazil.

The government's startling new approach came from the
city's desire to deal with pollution on all levels beyond its serious
problems with noise, air, and water pollution.

In 2006 São Paulo passed the Clean City Law, which banned
all outdoor advertising in Brazil's largest city. Over the course of
the next year, every single one of São Paulo's fifteen thousand
billboards, outdoor video screens, and bus advertisements vanished. With the elimination of the ads, the city beneath was laid
bare—a jungle of concrete buildings interspersed with stunning
historic architecture.

Brazil, as a country, is no stranger to controversial and innovative social and economic practices. In the 1940s, '50s, and '60s, the Brazilian government took extreme actions to reduce the country's dependence on imported foreign manufactured goods. This was a time when much of Brazil lacked a modern economic manufacturing infrastructure. The lack of domestically produced products left them stifled and struggling to become a modern economic nation; too much of their wealth left the country to import modern manufactured goods. To remedy the infrastructure problem the government set quotas on certain imports and imposed such high tariffs that it made it very uncomfortable, if not impossible, for Brazil's upper and business classes to have the modern conveniences they craved.

We decided that we should start combating pollution with the most conspicuous sector: visual pollution.
—Mayor Gilberto Kassab

The message sent to the Brazilian economic elite was simple: if you want fancy luxury items, then you have to invest in your own economy and build the infrastructure to make them yourself. It worked. These policies were the potent seeds of Brazil's current robust manufacturing economy, something rarely seen in postcolonial economies around the world, which tend to be dependent on modern imports at their own economic disadvantage.

Later, during the oil shocks of the 1970s, once again, in another bold effort to relieve foreign dependence—this time on foreign oil—Brazil expanded domestic oil production and other energy industry resources, leading to the creation of technology to produce sugarcane ethanol on a large scale. These efforts have resulted in the South American nation being one of the most energy-independent countries in the world today. It has surpassed most of its postcolonial economic pillagers in this way. So 2006's Clean City Law may have been shocking, but it was not at all that out of character for Brazil.

Digital, visual, and advertising pollution have been affecting us for more than a century now, diluting our personal voices and changing the way we interact with one another without most of us even recognizing it. It creeps up on us. It says a lot that São Paulo not only recognized the harm of it but audaciously did something about it.

After São Paulo implemented the Clean City Law, 70 percent of residents said the move had greatly improved quality of life in the city. The removal of the ads revealed a world of lost architecture and a calmer environment. The effort not only revealed long-covered buildings, it also revealed the city's long-standing poverty problems. Massive structures and edifices barren of advertising exposed many of the city's favelas (slums), many of which had long been hidden by billboards and signs.

When the ads came down, São Paulo natives first reported a feeling of disorientation. Mass messaging was such a part of the city's culture that billboards had become landmarks. "It's weird, because you get lost; you don't have any reference [points] any more," journalist Vinicius Galvão said in an interview with National Public Radio. In one part of town, the reporter had used a Panasonic billboard to orient himself. "But now my reference is an art deco building that was covered by this [massive Panasonic ad]," he recalled. "The city's now got new language; a new identity." Digital pollution, media pollution of any kind, vastly alters the way we see and identify with the world.

The elimination of ads in São Paulo uncovered a previously hidden world, which had been *diluted* due to content overload but that now shines forth its own new message. Ironically, the only compromise to the city's rigid outdoor advertising ban has been to allow approved graffiti and street art. The result has been a series of massive, iconic murals stretching the height of entire buildings. This is the city's true individual voice and expression: art and architecture—and the city can finally start to breathe as the distraction and dilution are vanquished.

Just like São Paulo's billboards hid the city's beauty (its historic architecture) and masked its poverty (the favelas), your message is similarly being hidden by the sheer volume and unrelenting force of digital communication (or pollution) today. When São Paulo made the city's slums clearly visible to all, more could be done about them. Similarly, when you understand and use Blocks you can essentially cause the overload of mass-messages to disappear from the mind of your intended audience, leaving just the individual message you want to convey.

POPULATIONS

3

The excessive increase of anything often causes
a reaction in the opposite direction.
—Plato, *Republic*

Like the city of São Paolo was crowded with billboards at the end of the twentieth
century, these days the world is a crowded place.

There is a concept in economics, taken from a 1798 essay by
English economist Thomas Robert Malthus, that argues the cor-
ollary relationship between population growth and food supply.
Malthus explains that population growth in humans is strongly
related to the amount of available food and sustenance.

For most of human history, our population grew steadily. But
relatively recent developments—innovations made within the
last three centuries—led to an explosion of populations. With
the onset of the First and Second Industrial Revolutions and
the emergence of mass production, an unprecedented capacity
to produce food facilitated a staggering growth in the world's
population. In recent years, the global population hit 7.5 billion
people. As recently as 150 years ago, this number would not have
been thought possible.

There are more people in the world than ever before—and that's led to previously unimaginable challenges that go far beyond food supply. When there is more of anything, the parts that make up the whole become less visible. (Kind of like if you had a puzzle with ten pieces versus ten thousand pieces.) Though you might not realize it, the exponential growth in global population is watering you down, making it far more difficult for you to stand out as an individual. Most of us can feel this.

A third revolution of digital technology has slammed us with messaging and communications without offering a constructive, healthy, balanced way of even attempting to *take it in*. Now, with this increase of billions and billions of people, these populations have a means of messaging at each other unceasingly, in real time, 24-7, 365 days a year. And they do. In many developing countries, even in villages with no running water, the people have smartphones.

With great irony, global *connectivity*, with ubiquitous all-the-time instant sharing, has left us more invisible and *isolated* than ever.

There are many reasons for this, as we'll see over the next few chapters. But the most obvious is the sheer volume of content out there—traditional media, social media, the news cycle, ads; it all adds up to make the world not only crowded but incredibly loud.

After the industrial revolutions of the nineteenth and early twentieth centuries came the Digital Revolution of the late twentieth. The world changed fast, and it keeps changing.

Fifty years ago, we only had three main broadcast networks—NBC, CBS, and ABC—so we watched what was put

WORLD POPULATION GROWTH

WORLD POPULATION GROWTH

POPULATION	YEAR	YEARS ELAPSED
1 MILLION	10K BC	
200 MILLION	0 AD	10,000
1 BILLION	1804	1,804
2 BILLION	1927	123
3 BILLION	1960	33
4 BILLION	1974	14
5 BILLION	1987	13
6 BILLION	1999	12
7 BILLION	2011	12
8 BILLION	2027	16
9 BILLION	2046	19

in front of us. Before cable TV took over, audiences were happy with their limited choices. Now we're living in an entertainment culture of "more, more, more!"

The proliferation of new media channels has created a vast need for content to fill pages and airwaves. Print magazines, online magazines, a mass of cable channels, broadcast networks, satellite radio channels, internet TV and radio stations, revolving billboards, and the endless array of other modern entertainment devices all need messages and content to share with their audiences.

It is not a surprise that such a ceaseless demand for content results in a *mass media industrial complex* and a desperate need to fill twenty-four hours of content across tens of thousands of mediums. This unthinking machine just keeps propelling itself forward, despite how inefficient it is, or its negative effects. In the race to get content out there, the speed at which it moves degrades the quality of the information—further weakening, if not destroying, the credibility of the information endlessly hurled at us.

Even with more information than ever vying for our attention, the businesses that create this onslaught continue to consolidate. Just six companies in the American media landscape own the major media outlets, from television to film production and distribution, as well as significant holdings across the globe in publishing, online communication, and more. Think about that . . . Six corporations own almost everything we listen to, watch, and read all over the world.

When you have this level of conglomeration, you run a risk of creating a series of echo chambers that stifle new thought, creativity, and innovation. The corporate interest striving to make a profit begins to define the type and nature of all content.

GLOBAL REACH OF MAJOR TV NEWS NETWORKS

CNN INTERNATIONAL (USA) 200+ COUNTRIES

BBC WORLD NEWS (UK) 200+ COUNTRIES

FRANCE 24 (FRANCE) 200+ COUNTRIES

211 COUNTRIES ON EARTH

AL JAZEERA (QATAR) 130+ COUNTRIES

This is where you get Fox News and CNN both echoing closely held beliefs to an existing audience of those who already agree with them. Publishing becomes a platform that serves primarily to amplify those with existing audiences, to guarantee a profit, leaving little room for new voices that may not have a platform. At a time when it is harder to get engagement than ever before, it is likely these echo chambers are the result of a choice to prioritize profitability, rather than the result of a desire to keep us informed. When you factor in advertising, the media noise becomes a cacophony. In the mid-2000s, the president of the marketing research firm Yankelovich, J. Walker-Smith, was widely quoted as saying that Americans had gone from seeing five hundred ads per day in the 1970s to as many as five thousand ads per day in 2006.

The explosion of social media and online advertising, among other developments, has confounded many researchers. Today, they won't even give a ballpark figure for the number of ads we are exposed to each day. (In 2015 Ron Marshall of Red Crow Marketing embarked on an interesting experiment. He decided to count how many ad messages he saw in a day. He got to 487 before finishing his breakfast! Bewildered and stunned, he decided to stop.) However, even if we didn't count the individual ads, one look at Google's advertising revenues from 2011 is a telling sign: the company earned $36.5 *billion* in advertising revenues that year, a 29 percent growth over the previous year. These are fees paid to Google to target you with an advertisement. This onslaught just continues to grow and grow at an astonishing rate.

Just like researchers, you can't even begin to calculate the number of ads you are exposed to each day, consciously or unconsciously. Advertising is just one small part of the competition for your attention online. There are also our social media vehicles,

THE BIG SIX

VIACOM

26
TV CABLE
NETWORKS

2
TV PRODUCTION
COMPANIES

10
TV BROADCAST
NETWORKS

170
INTERNATIONAL
TV NETWORKS

3
RADIO
STATIONS

7
FILM PRODUCTION
COMPANIES

1
MAGAZINE

2
MUSIC
PUBLISHERS

35
WEBSITES

DISNEY

7
TV
NETWORKS

26
TV CABLE
NETWORKS

8
OWNED &
OPERATED
TV STATIONS

226
ABC AFFILIATES

11
INTERNATIONAL
TV CHANNELS

12
PRODUCTION &
DISTRIBUTION
FILM COMPANIES

277
RADIO
STATIONS

30+
WEBSITES

16
BOOK
PUBLISHERS

6
MAGAZINES

5
MUSIC
PUBLISHERS

CBS

1
TV
NETWORK

19
TV CABLE
NETWORKS

16
OWNED &
OPERATED
TV STATIONS

200+
ABC AFFILIATES

5
INTERNATIONAL
TV CHANNELS

130
RADIO
STATIONS

25
WEBSITES

21
BOOK
PUBLISHERS

TIME WARNER

1
TV BROADCAST
NETWORK

25
TV CABLE
NETWORKS

13
TV PRODUCTION
& DISTRIBUTION
COMPANIES

11
REGIONAL/
LOCAL CHANNELS

27
INTERNATIONAL
TV NETWORKS

9
FILM PRODUCTION
& DISTRIBUTION
COMPANIES

150+
MAGAZINES

25+
WEBSITES

2
COMIC BOOK
PUBLISHERS

30
BOOK
PUBLISHERS

NEWS CORP

2
TV
NETWORKS

37
TV CABLE
NETWORKS

25
OWNED &
OPERATED
TV STATIONS

226
FOX AFFILIATES

11
SATELLITE
TV NETWORKS

46
INTERNATIONAL
TV NETWORKS

15
FILM PRODUCTION
& DISTRIBUTION
COMPANIES

150+
NEWSPAPERS

35
WEBSITES

2
BOOK
PUBLISHERS

30
MAGAZINES

GENERAL ELECTRIC

3
TV
NETWORKS

29
TV CABLE
NETWORKS

10
OWNED &
OPERATED
TV STATIONS

200+
NBC AFFILIATES

14
INTERNATIONAL
TV CHANNELS

4
TV PRODUCTION
& DISTRIBUTION
COMPANIES

3
FILM PRODUCTION
& DISTRIBUTION
COMPANIES

11
PARTNERSHIPS WITH
OTHER PRODUCTION
COMPANIES

20+
WEBSITES

1
MAGAZINE

including Twitter feeds, Facebook feeds, Pinterest, Instagram, and all the other content that is blasted at us in ad-like fashion. If you include these mediums, we are looking at possibly tens of thousands of micromessages pummeling us every day, nonstop. Technology is, simply put, exhausting.

The amount of data that now exists is difficult to grasp. A *Science* article put it in interesting (if still mind-boggling) terms: if we put all the stored electronic data existing on the planet on CDs and placed them on top of each other, one thin 1.2 millimeter disk on top of another, that stack of CDs would reach beyond the moon.

Since we're talking in CDs—a nearly shelved technology on its way out—think of how many CDs worth of music, or photos, your smartphone holds. Mind-blowing. Despite how much digital content we are able to hold in our devices, there is now almost more data in the world than there are the mainframes to store it. There is just more stuff in the world than we can handle, and it is growing every day. In 2012 we were storing 1,750 exabytes of data. It is predicted, according to that same *Science* article, that this amount will explode up to 40,000 exabytes by 2020.

To put this in perspective, think of this: just five exabytes is the equivalent of every word ever spoken by human beings since the dawn of humankind. That should give you a sense of the sheer blithering volume of a single exabyte.

As consumers we're always wired up, jacked in, and overloaded. This is truly a dramatic shift considering that just a hundred years ago, we had the printed word, the theater, and possibly the radio as our only available sources of "media stimulation" within our homes. A couple of decades after that, television became widespread. Now, several decades after the invention of the internet, we have a meteor shower of

ADS SEEN PER DAY BY AVERAGE AMERICANS

1970
500

TODAY

5,000

AMOUNT OF DIGITAL INFORMATION ON EARTH

YEAR	EXABYTES
2006	150
2007	200
2008	250
2009	500
2010	750
2011	1,200
2012	1,750
2020	40,000

Source: "What's a Zettabyte? By 2015, the Internet Will Know, Says Cisco," *Charles Arthur*, Guardian, *June 9, 2011.*

technology-driven choices raining down on us. And more is not better, especially in the case of cell phones being everywhere. The title of a research article from the University of Chicago Press speaks for itself: "Brain Drain: The Mere Presence of One's Own Smartphone Reduces Available Cognitive Capacity." Just by having the slightest bit of attention on our phone we reduce our capacity to think. Or, as an article in the *Atlantic* put it, "Your Smartphone Reduces Your Brainpower, Even if It's Just Sitting There." Yes, our cell phones make us dumber just by their presence . . . we don't even have to be using them.

While web search engines purport to help us sort through the massive amounts of information thrown at us, they actually compound the problem. Think about your last Google search. How many results did you get? Tens of thousands? Millions?

Yet every time we click a web link, we take for granted that the programmers behind the search engines have analytics and algorithms that put the best results on the first page. But when you get a hundred million search results from a single query, it shows you the weakness of having so many options. Are you ever going to check beyond the first ten or first fifty, let alone the top one hundred? And yet there's always a shadow of a doubt: *Has the search algorithm really delivered to us the best of what's out there?*

In a BBC article, reporter Ruth Alexander highlights how Google autofills our searches as we type, leading us to popular searches, thus making those terms even more popular. She gives the example of what happens when she searches her own name in Google and gets over sixty-eight million results, even though, in her words, "I've written no books, starred in no films, and you've probably never heard of me. And yet I'm massive on the web." Alexander goes on to say, "Even when you've got your enquiry honed to a fine degree, and consider yourself a champion in Google-fu, don't believe the numbers."

Imagine a golf ball is an advertisement or social media message. Now, imagine that a golf ball is lightly tossed at you every thirty seconds. You could easily catch every single one. What if ten thousand golf balls were tossed at you all at once? You would brace yourself or even curl up like a baby. You would turn away and try to avoid the balls. This is just what this digital, visual, and advertising pollution does. It overwhelms us, distracts us, dilutes our voices, and greatly weakens our ability to focus and make decisions.

This is the world you are trying to message to and get attention in. It's not just you. In a world where those around you are constantly distracted, you are now invisible.

FORCE FIELDS

4

The Rejection of Mass Information

Life is denied by lack of attention, whether it be to cleaning windows or trying to write a masterpiece.
—**Nadia Boulanger**

See if this all-too-common scenario seems familiar: You're trying to have a focused video chat with a coworker in another city, but there's a call to your mobile phone on hold, and then a Facebook status alert flashes on the screen, making you wonder if you have updated your social networks. From there, your mind wanders to whether your DVR is recording your favorite show, and if you've checked in with your spouse lately, or spent any time with your kids—let alone called your parents—or met up with that college friend you've been promising to get together with, or paid any of the e-bills coming due on your bank account this month . . . All those messages distract you, to some degree, from each person or activity. Each engagement suffers from hijacked and decreased attention.

The immediate and important ideas, people, and interests in your life still get your focused attention, but you likely perceive them far less clearly because of all the added distractions.

When there is something necessary to our immediate survival—
something that turns on our fight-or-flight impulses—we will be
highly perceptive and take in everything around us. But most of
the time we communicate in small increments like email, texts,
instant messages, and quick mobile calls. All these ever-growing
micromessaging platforms from Messenger to WhatsApp and
beyond have created a huge cultural shift, causing us to communicate, more than ever before, in brief spurts.

In the 1980s and '90s a tech executive named Linda Stone
worked for both Apple and Microsoft in the field of emerging
technologies. By 1998 Stone had come up with the phrase "continuous partial attention" to describe the new human experience
of how most of us are so overwhelmed by input that we're paying
increasingly less attention to our environment and all the messaging that comes in, to the point where we don't fully engage
with anything anymore.

*I've just opened my email and there's nothing out
of the ordinary there. It's the usual daily flood of
schedule, project, travel, information, and junk
mail. Then I notice . . . I'm holding my breath.
—Linda Stone on the phenomenon she called "email
apnea," a temporary absence or suspension of
breathing, or shallow breathing, while doing email*

What's fascinating is that Stone did this study during the
burgeoning days of the internet, almost a full decade before the
tumultuous barrage of social media that now continually inter-
rupts us. So if it was true that getting attention was hard in the
mid- to late '90s, what does it say about the attention spans of
those we are trying to talk to today?

MOST MOBILE PHONE USE WORLDWIDE

CHINA	INDIA	USA
963 MILLION USERS	**884** MILLION USERS	**323** MILLION USERS
71% OF POPULATION	**73%** OF POPULATION	**102%** OF POPULATION

Source: "Cell Phone Usage Worldwide, by Country," Infoplease.
© 2000–2017 Sandbox Networks, Inc.

PERCENTAGE OF AMERICANS WITH...

	50 YEARS AGO	TODAY
MOBILE PHONES	**0%**	**85%**
INTERNET ACCESS	**0%**	**78%**
DESKTOP/ LAPTOP COMPUTERS	**0%**	**76%**
MP3 PLAYERS	**0%**	**47%**
GAME CONSOLES	**0%**	**42%**
TABLETS/ E-READERS	**0%**	**9%**

Source: "Three Technology Revolutions," Pew Research Center, retrieved February 2014.

We have been transformed abruptly in only fifty years. This change has occurred almost instantly, and the change is especially striking if you look at how dramatically it has altered all of our lives so rapidly. Of course, the Second Industrial Revolution (mass production, the invention of the electric lightbulb, the assembly-line engine, and the advent of cars) also changed us. But the internet is different in how it has affected us internally, in ways we don't fully understand. We can see machines like cars and electric lights in front of us. We cannot "see" the internet and its effects are far more profound. From where we were fifty years ago to now is a flip of a light switch in terms of the passage of time.

We are culturally trying to catch up and figure out how this brave new digital world is affecting all of us.

We all want ways to lower the volume. But in our quest to reduce the onslaught, we turn yet again to technology—spam folders, DVRs, pop-up blockers, satellite radio, and subscription-based news feeds—to screen out the junk we don't want to see. In essence, we're creating a merry-go-round of technological interdependence: we develop technology to make our lives easier and more effective, then we get overwhelmed by it, and we develop new technologies to screen out the ones we originally created.

How many times has a friend or family member not heard what you said because they were distracted by technology? It's a cliché. We all know people tend to fixate on their devices when they are texting, browsing the web, or scanning social media feeds. Before you know it, they're deep in an electronic trance. The satirical news website the *Onion* hilariously but profoundly highlighted this disconnect in a piece posted on Christmas Day in 2013. The headline read, "Relatives Gather from Across the Country to Stare into Screens Together."

WORLDWIDE PHONE PROLIFERATION

	MOBILE PHONE SUBSCRIPTIONS	% OF POPULATION
GLOBAL	5.98 BILLION	87%
DEVELOPED NATIONS	1.46 BILLION	118%
DEVELOPING	4.52	

ASIA & PACIFIC — **2.9** BILLION

AFRICA — **433** MILLION

ARAB STATES — **349** MILLION

CIS (formerly the USSR) — **399** MILLION

EUROPE — **741** MILLION

THE AMERICAS — **969** MILLION

Source: International Telecommunications Union Key Information and Communication Technology Data, 2005–2017.

The *Onion* went on to quote a fictional twenty-eight-year-old as saying, "It's just great to get home for a while and spend some quality time not speaking a single word to my relatives, whether that's by sipping hot cocoa with my sister while we both check our emails, or by gathering the whole clan for a nice holiday meal where everyone is fixedly looking down at the text messages on their phones—'tis the season, you know?"

While the "fictional" article pokes gentle fun at our technological obsession, we definitely notice when people around us mentally check out and lock into their gadgets, detaching from the world around them, which includes us. How can we possibly get the attention we need to thrive with consistency in a ridiculous world like this?

In our contemporary society we have become used to receiving small bits or micropieces of information as the normal way to perceive information. This means that our technological world is encouraging shorter and shorter attention spans. But as all of this microinformation pummels us, we have simultaneously, on some level, become desensitized to the messages constantly coming at us, because there are just too many of them.

The result is a tricky and cumbersome albatross that we have become unwittingly accustomed to shouldering. We rely on microbursts (advertising as well as text messages, email, and other short-form communication)—but at the same time, we subconsciously repel it reflexively. The ubiquity of DVRs and ad-free satellite radio services reveals our true feelings about advertising. You can also see it with simple spam filters and other advertising-avoidance technologies, which have swelled into multibillion-dollar industries. We are repulsed by being overpromoted to.

Even with this, certain media (like print magazines, billboards, etc.) can't be caught with spam filters. That means we solve the problem of too much information by developing our own internal ad blockers. Most of us are now simply numb to many ads. We're not only distracted; we're desensitized. Also, we associate most unsolicited media messages with too much hype or dishonesty, and we react with disinterest or repulsion—we don't take notice or we look away.

What is the flip side of that reflexive overload survival mechanism? Well, we now filter out so much information that we wind up missing out on materials and experiences that could be valuable to us.

If Einstein were alive, he'd wake up tomorrow and spend the first couple hours of his day digging out his inbox and getting a bunch of Slack notifications. And we wouldn't have relativity.
—Drew Houston, founder and CEO, Dropbox

Our brains often don't distinguish between a microburst that's carrying useful information and one that's purely promotional. In our minds, we're overwhelmed and we check out. At some point during the rise of social media and mobile devices, we became more resistant and desensitized to all types of micro-communication in our environment—including the individual voices that we actually need to hear.

As we have gotten accustomed to shorter and shorter pieces of information, it has become difficult for us to concentrate on more complex, large bodies of information. So here we are: socially conditioned to the point where we are used to taking in tiny bits of data, while at the same time using our mental spam filters to subconsciously repel short or tiny bursts of data.

The effects of this catch-22 are maddening to marketers and almost catastrophic in the field of education. The paradox also has a huge social impact because our filtering mechanisms make it harder and harder for us to listen to one another in our day-to-day lives, both personally and professionally.

This problem is further intensified by the fact that complex, intricate pieces of information are necessary not only to communicate our ideas but for our world to function. Doctors, nurses, engineers, scientists, artists, and business managers all need to share and receive complicated information to innovate, learn, and ensure our society runs smoothly.

As more and more of our time is consumed by this barrage of content that we think is connecting us, we actually have less time in the day to talk to each other in any concentrated way. This is *The Iconist*'s **paradox**: *we communicate more and more with micro-communication, but at the same time we have become desensitized to it and filter most of it out.* Even your close personal relationships could be improved by first just understanding our natural repulsion to content overload. You can choose to take the time to shut off devices and connect in a deeper way.

All of this digital interaction also makes us feel like some task is always left unfinished or not fully examined. There's always more to do in a world with twenty-four-hour data connections and round-the-clock media broadcasts. But the greater cost is this: your ability to be seen and differentiate yourself has been seriously diminished and it happened fast. Mass distraction really does mean invisibility for the individual human. Like drops of rain in the ocean, our voices are being diluted.

LIGHTS OUT

5

The Dilution Effect

Not till we are lost, in other words not till we have
lost the world, do we begin to find ourselves.
—**Henry David Thoreau,** *Walden*

In January 2011 TV network FX premiered an innovative new show. *Lights Out*
starred Holt McCallany as Patrick "Lights" Leary, a former
world heavyweight boxing champion who suffers from pugilistic
dementia as a result of being hit in the head too many times.
Because of his condition, he is forced to go to work for the mob
to continue to support his family. The show was gritty and flashy.
It was also the first weekly TV drama about the day-to-day life of
a world champion boxer. It showcased flamboyant subject matter with delicate and complex characters.

Dozens of newspapers, entertainment magazines, and websites hailed it as one of the best television shows in years. The
Hollywood Reporter loaded its review with superlatives. TV critic
Tim Goodman called the show one of the most compelling
dramas on TV and praised Holt McCallany, a longtime character actor, in a "'where-did-this-guy-come-from,' star-making,

breakout role." "In his virtuoso performance, [McCallany is] able to elevate the series and give 'Lights' Leary more shape and substance than anyone could have expected," Goodman wrote. "It's a monster performance with both subtlety and power. You can't take your eyes off McCallany, and in turn, *Lights Out* has a hook that comes out of nowhere."

More than a dozen other reviewers echoed Goodman's sentiments, calling the series terrific and the cast outstanding and giving McCallany praise for his powerhouse performance. But the ratings went through ups and downs. So despite the show's rave reviews and universal praise for its charismatic lead, the critically acclaimed series was canceled after just one season.

Now, a show that's lauded by critics but fails in its first season is, unfortunately for those who worked on it, not that uncommon. But a television executive being as candid as John Landgraf, the president of FX Networks, just might be. Landgraf is known for being exceedingly honest with fans and journalists alike, and this is what he had to say about canceling a show that he green-lit and personally loved:

> No matter how good the show is, the question is, are they
> somebody's first choice? Are they good enough . . . I looked
> at the tracking data. In January and February, there are 18
> new original series premiering on cable. There are another 18
> returning series launching on cable and 16 new and returning
> series launching on broadcast networks. That's 52 original
> series premiering in January and February alone. You have to
> think about the competitive environment on the night *Lights
> Out* premiered . . . Getting traction with something new
> and something different has gotten devilishly hard . . . It's
> become tougher and tougher to find a slot to wiggle through if

you're trying to make something competitively excellent, and different, that isn't just designed to be noisy and shocking.

The ratings leader on the night that *Lights Out* premiered was MTV's noisy, shocking reality hit *Teen Mom*.

Lead actor McCallany reflects on that time, "It was a difficult moment. I knew John liked the show, he often said very complimentary things about the show, and about my performance . . . but we were failing to gather enough attention. It was especially hard because it was my first true starring role, after twenty years in the business, so I'd have done anything to see the show succeed."

It would be hard for anyone to get such praise and still fail.

According to John Landgraf's research department, FX Research, there were over four hundred scripted shows slated for 2015 and an estimate of close to five hundred in 2017. The number just keeps going up and up. (And it's worth keeping in mind that the fifty-two new or original series Landgraf mentioned did not include all the reality shows, documentary series, webisodes, podcasts, and the millions of hours of instantly available videos on YouTube.)

Yet in 2018, despite this crushing setback, McCallany emerged as the star of one of Netflix's most watched *and* critically praised shows of the year, *Mindhunter*, directed by David Fincher. This show was master director Fincher's second television show. The director—who has directed music videos for many eminent artists as well as films including *Se7en* and *The Social Network*—had given McCallany his first major role twenty-five years earlier in Fincher's feature film directorial debut, *Alien 3*.

Despite the failure of *Lights Out* as a series, all the press and adoration lavished upon Holt in the popular press likely imbued

Fincher and the network with confidence that he could carry his own show and helped sell him to the network as a bankable leading man. The torrent of press praising McCallany's formidable and unorthodox performance served as a powerful Block driving the now-middle-aged actor far beyond a journeyman's career, to great heights. He is now consistently considered among Hollywood's elite, in demand for the roles every young actor dreams about.

McCallany says about his life now, "It makes me very grateful for the success . . . on *Mindhunter*. I know what it's like to have the other experience. Famed boxing trainer Teddy Atlas once said to me, 'The most important thing is not how long it takes a man to get to his destination, the most important thing is that he gets there.'"

People are important, and what they do in their lives is important. Dilution works against us, but like McCallany, we can all rise above and succeed.

The sheer volume of noise dilutes the power of any individual message. Think of it like a chemical reaction where the power of the reaction is directly proportional to the potency of the reactive chemicals being used. Dilute the chemicals and you lessen the intensity of the reaction between the substances involved. This is what dilution does to our human experience. It makes it weaker. It lessens it. It decreases the power of who we are.

Think about Linda Stone's concept of "continuous partial attention," which says that as our attention is constantly divided we cease engaging deeply. We often relate to this idea in purely selfish terms, as we, ourselves, feel so constantly distracted and pulled this way and that way by mass messaging, electronic devices, and whirling choice overload. When we are overloaded with too much of something, we reject it.

What we often don't think about is what this new way of interfacing with the world is doing to those who are trying to reach *us*. And, relatedly, what that means about our own ability to have a voice and be heard. If those around us are only *partially* paying attention, rejecting what is coming at them, then those of us trying to engage with them and get their attention are not really being heard anymore. Thus, artists, professionals, entrepreneurs, we're all diluted, pitted against ever-increasing content, while those we are trying to reach have ever-*decreasing* attention. And we can feel it.

No matter our vocation in life, all of us must find our own ways to be noticed against a backdrop of constant interference, and be seen by an audience that's constantly distracted. Again, it hasn't always been so hard for talented people, smart ideas, or good products to stand out. Being overwhelmed by more than we can consume—for McCallany, as for most of us—has metaphorically turned the *lights out* and we are often left in the dark, struggling to be seen.

Even when we actively seek connection, even love, technology-driven choices bring us together while simultaneously pushing us apart. When there are simply too many options, intensity of connection is destroyed. In a 2013 *New Yorker* magazine article on the profound social shift toward online dating, author Ann Friedman points out how easy it is to be dismissive of the abundance of dating profiles. Dating has become more and more like shopping in a supermarket. In her article she demonstrates why users continue to scroll without ever stopping to learn more about a potential partner, ultimately turning dating into a process of sifting through "products" in a distant and detached way.

From the online dating searcher's perspective, Friedman writes:

> Ignore; ignore. I'm seeing so many men with questionable facial hair that I double-check my profile to make sure that I haven't accidentally indicated a preference for goatees. [Unsolicited messages cause me to] scream and toss the phone to the other end of the couch, as if this action will repel the men within it. Even though I know these men can't see my exact location, I feel cornered, overwhelmed.

Human beings start to become as interchangeable as chocolate bars in a vending machine or breakfast cereal boxes in a supermarket aisle. We stop at the first sugary snack that catches our eye and ignore the alternatives. When there is so much, we simply don't engage in a serious way. Looking for a life partner should probably be a more focused and specific activity. But as they say, don't hate the player, hate the game.

The number of online dating profiles is staggering. If you have one of those profiles, once again, you're being diluted. Whether you're browsing to select a date or posting a profile in hopes someone else will select it, it's depressing for both parties because you're seeking a human connection in a place where finding it, at least as far as deep connection goes, seems impossible. When it is so easy to interact with others superficially, we can become lazy when bumping into people one-on-one in the physical world where we might be able to go a little deeper.

It is a testament to the resilience of the human spirit that millions of people do actually find each other online.

THE DILUTION CLOUD

VERY LITTLE BREAKS THROUGH

MORE RESISTANCE

MORE SENDERS

RECEIVERS

SENDERS

On some level, everyone feels like Friedman or one of those eligible bachelors: How can I connect to the right person? What's wrong with me? We take the anxiety from these thoughts and experiences into the world with us, and the next time we are in a crowd, we think to ourselves: "Am I just another face to swipe, or box to tick, or distraction to ignore?" And when you think about how many selection processes you have to go through in a day, week, or month, on the endless list of things that we do in life, all that time adds up. Dilution = emotional, mental, and physical exhaustion.

In our current theater of too much of everything, standing out has more often to do with the ability to be seen and heard than talent, luck, or skill.

INVISIBLE MAN

6

I am an invisible man . . . I am a man of substance, of
flesh and bone, fiber and liquids—and I might even
be said to possess a mind. I am invisible, understand,
simply because people refuse to see me.
—**Ralph Ellison**, *Invisible Man*

We all know someone whose success confounds us: the mediocre actor, the
incompetent boss, the tone-deaf pop star, the bumbling politi-
cian. We watch them succeed, furrow our brows, and ask, "Why
them?"

Most of us think that our ultimate success has to do with
a combination of talent, hard work, intelligence, organization,
charisma, and luck. (Charm and good looks don't hurt, either.)
We believe that if we have enough of these characteristics, and
work hard enough and with enough intensity, we'll get what we
want. Yet the truth is that these factors often have less to do with
success than you might think. Achieving your goals has more to
do with your ability to stand out from the crowd and ensure that
your message is heard.

In our media-saturated society, it is a talent unto itself to be
able to stand out. No matter how talented you are, if you aren't

being heard in a credible way, you will fail. On the other hand, a less talented person who can stand out and grab attention will often be successful. The ubiquity of many reality TV stars proves this daily.

Imagine what it was like to hunt for a job just twenty-five years ago. We looked in the newspaper classifieds and maybe saw some sort of recruiter to narrow our options, but we were ultimately limited by the number of places we could look for employment. Today, you have tens of thousands of options through a slew of employment websites. This is more ominous than comforting and job-hunters actually experience increased anxiety as they attempt to go through all the choices and figure out the best places to apply.

This is also true for employers and HR departments, which now get more applications than they could possibly read or call in for an interview, leaving employers with the uneasy feeling that they might be missing out on that one "right" person. What seems like a boon in opportunity is, in reality, a dubious blessing. Job-hunting is a much more difficult process compared to when we only had classified ads and recruitment agencies—the competition is fierce.

As many in the American workforce can attest, extended periods of joblessness are not just financially difficult but powerfully disillusioning and even disturbing. There have been news reports about the middle-aged man in the Midwest who has stuck to his routine of logging on to his computer every morning to doggedly search for jobs online day after day. How does this guy feel after five months go by without finding a job? What about when he hits the ten-, twelve-, or twenty-four-month mark?

An informal online poll by CNBC showed the average American's perception of job websites.

PEOPLE WHO THINK CAREER WEBSITES ARE A GOOD PLACE TO FIND A JOB

YES
29%

NO
71%

NUMBER OF JOB APPLICANTS AT A MAJOR U.S. COMPANY

JOB APPLICANTS

1,000,000

NEW HIRES FROM ONLINE APPLICATIONS

LESS THAN 1%

Source: Lou Adler, "This Single Job Hunting Statistic Will Blow Your Mind," LinkedIn, June 28, 2016, www.linkedin.com/pulse/single-job -hunting-statistic-blow-your-mind-lou-adler, accessed June 12, 2019.

Surprisingly, the actual statistics are far worse than the perception, which is already pretty bad.

Several recent statistics from large companies show that millions of people apply online each year for a very limited number of job openings, which means your actual chances of getting a job are far, far less than 1 percent.

As the American economy slid in the late 2000s, like many previous smaller dips before it, tens of millions of people turned to online job listings and career sites to find work, and the portals like CareerBuilder, Monster, Yahoo!, HotJobs, and Indeed have reaped the benefits, making billions of dollars. But how many people do you know who have actually gotten an interview, let alone a job, after applying through an online job board?

The feeling of being a lost résumé in a haystack of applicants would be beyond frustrating and even mind-numbing if you're already struggling to make ends meet. Even if you're not on your last rung, the mental effect of shouting out your hopes into the endless cosmos of the web where no one may actually be listening would create anxiety, depression, numbness, paralysis, and apathy in most. What's scary here is that the already doubtful promise does not match the reality when it comes down to your actual chances of finding a job online. The perpetrator is dilution and it's really quite depressing to think about.

The bizarre reality is that as much as technology helps us find employment opportunities, it also weakens our chances to secure a new job.

Job searching is an obvious, palpable example, but in every area of life we are forced to sell ourselves, our ideas, and our work. Artists of every kind often feel this frustration in the deepest of ways. More of everything continues to water us down as individuals, diluting our voices. In other words, when we know we are competing against a sea of content and other applicants, we can't help but feel small. The awareness of our own insignificance is like a bass note that beats constantly through our lives—we may not consciously hear it, but we can feel it.

A need for personal esteem is a universal human urge. We have an innate need to individually define, express, and differentiate ourselves from others. Psychologist Abraham Maslow explains through his hierarchy of needs that after we get our basic physiological necessities (food, air, and sleep) and safety needs (shelter, safe environments) met, the next two needs in the pyramid—social belonging and esteem—relate to kinds of recognition. The blow to our self-esteem when we can't find work is a gut-wrenching example of how almost anyone can be damaged when he or she feels watered down and diluted to the point of invisibility.

When we feel we don't have a voice, we're *miserable*. It takes a toll on us emotionally, manifesting itself in a variety of ways, including escapism, addiction, and mental instability. If you take an extreme example of solitary confinement in prisons, many studies have shown that lack of human contact has dire psychological consequences. In 2012 the American Psychological Association published an assessment of studies chronicling the severe psychological effects of solitary confinement. The studies show the mental effects of extended deprivation of human contact: anxiety, panic, insomnia, paranoia, aggression, and depression. All of these would lead to forms of escapism, addiction, and a traumatized mental outlook.

Now, solitary confinement is an extreme form of isolation, but the digital world does isolate us and I would argue that it has a related (if subtler) effect. We all react differently to varying degrees of isolation, but it is not too much of a leap to understand that reduced human contact through increased digital connection would have a negative effect. In a 2003 article for *Crime & Delinquency*, Craig Haney writes, "It borders on being common sense, but it's common sense with a lot of empirical research that supports it . . . So much of what we do and who we are is rooted in a social context."

When we feel isolated, we often feel like we cannot accomplish our personal goals. We feel like there's nothing we can do to make ourselves heard. The fact is, the ability to stand out goes far beyond talent and hard work—it has a lot to do with our long-term emotional durability and confidence. If we feel harshly broken by dilution, many of us won't get up and try again and will just end up feeling even more isolated, our voices even more diluted.

The people who stand out are the ones that succeed, while those who don't get seen, no matter how amazing they are, fail. We all know this in our bones, yet we rarely think about the internal effect it has on us. Our ability to express ourselves is a huge factor that contributes to our sense of self-worth and well-being.

Getting past the obstacle of information overload and standing out above the competition is not just about how you convey information. Rather, it's about understanding how other human beings prefer to take in information. Icons—bold, oversimplified imagery or repetitive statements—are how others most prefer to take in the world around them.

To become a successful Iconist you have to understand and believe that standing out is equal to if not more important than talent, at least as far as widespread success is concerned. History is littered with hardworking, brilliant people who died unknown and with pennies in their pockets because they did not find a way for their talents to be seen.

THE AMERICAN GANGSTER

7

Be daring, be different, be impractical, be anything
that will assert integrity of purpose and imaginative
vision against the play-it-safers, the creatures of
the commonplace, the slaves of the ordinary.
—Cecil Beaton

Chael Sonnen is an unusual mixed martial artist and cage fighter who lives in the
Pacific Northwest. He represents the other side of dilution: what
being seen, combined with hard work and raw talent, can do.

For nearly a decade, Sonnen languished in the middle ranks
of mixed martial arts (MMA) while competing in a cluster of
small fight organizations. Eventually, MMA's popularity grew and
it became mainstream. In the mid-2000s the Ultimate Fighting
Championship (UFC) emerged as the premier MMA promotion
company and served as a catalyst for what was becoming one of
the fastest-growing sports in the world as MMA gyms popped up
by the thousands all over the United States.

A powerful All-American wrestler from the University of
Oregon, Sonnen won the Greco-Roman silver medal at the

2000 World University Championships in Tokyo. Despite his college success and physical talent, as an MMA fighter he never seemed to get recognized as an elite world-class talent, perhaps because, as the sport grew, it became hard to stand out. Sonnen pressed forward as a journeyman for nearly a decade.

MMA involves every martial arts discipline—including wrestling, Thai kickboxing, boxing, and jujitsu, a Brazilian variation of Japanese combat techniques—consisting of a highly evolved form of grappling, physical holds, chokes, and submissions that aim to get your opponent to "tap out" in defeat. When the sport reached a new peak of popularity in 2010, Sonnen was thirty-three, an age at which many fighters face the twilight of their careers. But between 2010 and 2012, he reinvented himself, resulting in a resurgence the like of which is rarely, if ever, seen in any professional sport.

In just three years, Sonnen competed in three UFC championship fights in two different weight classes and became one of the premier fighters in the sport, transforming himself into an international superstar. He also became one of the top five income-producing draws for the UFC during televised pay-per-view bouts. Amazingly, at least at the time, he was the only MMA fighter who was not a sitting or former champion to achieve this level of success.

Did you get that? He was always a competitor but *never* a champion and was one of the top MMA draws of all time. So why were so many people interested in watching him?

The simple answer is, Sonnen started talking. He started using his quick, poetic, and sometimes brutal mind to promote his fights. And when he did, a startling thing happened. He got credit for his athleticism in ways he never had before. His impact was no longer diluted. Despite his failure to achieve a gold UFC championship belt, he became, at age thirty-five, known as the best wrestler in MMA. (He'd later become infamous for other reasons.)

Sonnen's talent was always there, so how come he never got credit for it? Everything changed for him after he participated in a series of controversial interviews and appearances. He spoke spontaneously and defiantly, breaking from the crowd with his candor about two of the most respected and beloved MMA fighters in Brazil—twin brothers Rogério and Rodrigo Nogueira:

> I was in Las Vegas when the Nogueira brothers first touched down in America. There was a bus—this is a true story. There was a bus that pulled up to a red light and the little Nog tried to feed it a carrot while the big Nog was petting it. He thought it was a horse. This really happened. He tried to feed a bus a carrot and now you are telling me this country has computers? I didn't know that.

He didn't make any friends in Brazil when the story went viral and became water-cooler fodder for MMA fans worldwide. Sonnen stood out, and people listened. Fans of the fastest-growing sport in the world hung on his every word and, love him or hate him, they wanted to know the next thing that was going to come out of his mouth. His interviews and press conferences became an event. Chael seemed to always have something interesting to deliver.

One of his most memorable quotes took on the taboo subject of religion:

> You know people want to talk about God: "Oh, I want to thank God." Listen, I'm a God-fearing man, go to church every

Sunday and have since I was a boy. But if I ever found out that God cared one way or the other about a borderline illegal fist fight on Saturday night [referring to his battles in the UFC Octagon], I would be greatly disappointed and it would make me rethink my entire belief system.

Despite criticism, Sonnen repeated his antics anywhere people or the press were paying attention. He made TV appearances where he carried a fake UFC gold belt and claimed to be the champion of the sport. Yes, his behavior made some hate him, but it also made him a fan favorite because he was a larger-than-life personality, a self-proclaimed "American gangster from West Linn, Oregon."

Chael rarely, if ever, broke character. He had no problem saying that Anderson Silva, whom many consider to be the greatest MMA fighter of all time, "sucked." This was at a time when there was an almost spiritual reverence for Silva in the sport, as he never lost and beat his opponents in ways that were often cinematic. Silva beat everyone that was thrown at him for years, and he made it look easy.

Chael's mischief resulted in a media frenzy where he quickly became one of the most talked-about athletes in the world, especially outside the United States where MMA enjoys tremendous popularity. Chael Sonnen got TV hosting and analyst opportunities outside the cage as a direct result of talking and grabbing attention.

Because Sonnen had the skill and athleticism to back up his taunts, he only narrowly lost the first bout to legendary champion Silva by making a fluke mistake. He eventually had two epic fights with Anderson Silva and, at the time, pulled in record pay-per-view revenue for the UFC. The historic two fights between Anderson and Chael were the subject of a feature-length documentary produced by Anderson Silva himself, where he painted Chael as his nemesis and greatest rival. There was a second short documentary film produced about this rivalry by hip-hop icon and artist Jay Z.

Popular sports host Jim Rome has quipped, "Chael Sonnen is the best trash talker in all of sports," while UFC president Dana White commented, "I've never seen anyone who can talk like this guy can since Muhammad Ali." Sonnen's honest, thoughtful, yet outrageous comments eventually resulted in a book deal, Chael Sonnen's *The Voice of Reason: A VIP Pass to Enlightenment*.

It is not likely that Chael engaged in any of his antics as cavalierly as he often liked to portray. Chael got a degree in sociology while wrestling at the University of Oregon and, at times, referenced it when interviewers accused him of purely having a big mouth. According to his jujitsu coach for the Anderson fights, Scott McQuary, it should come as no surprise that Chael's childhood heroes were Muhammad Ali and Mr. T.

"Braggin" is when a person says something and can't do it. I do what I say.
—Muhammad Ali

YouTube users created dozens of videos dedicated to highlighting Chael's bold statements and entertaining ways as his celebrity grew. It was easy to see what had happened—he had talked his way into two successive title fights, and in doing so, he had made a lot more money than many others in the sport.

Dan Henderson, one of his closest friends and a former world champion MMA fighter, said in an interview, "I guess I should just quit training to win fights . . . and go to shit talking school." Fighters and championship contenders Phil Davis and Shane Carwin echoed the sentiment, coming forward to say that they would attend that school.

A few years before Lance Armstrong famously admitted on Oprah Winfrey's couch that he used performance-enhancing drugs, Sonnen called out the cycling icon for hypocrisy:

> Take Lance Armstrong. Lance Armstrong did a number of things and he gave himself cancer. He cheated, he did drugs, and he gave himself cancer. Well, instead of saying, "Hey listen, I cheated and gave myself cancer—don't be like me," he went out and profited something like 15 million from this "Hey, poor me—let's find a cure for cancer" campaign instead of just coming clean and saying, "Look, here's what I did. I screwed myself up and hope people learn from my mistakes."

Sonnen was vilified for attacking an American hero at the time, but he got a lot of attention, particularly from outraged cancer survivors who had been inspired by Armstrong's Livestrong Foundation. But his comments about Armstrong foreshadowed the fighter's own mea culpa. In 2014 Sonnen himself tested positive for performance-enhancing drugs three times, earning a two-year ban from fighting and getting fired from a high-profile MMA analyst job with Fox Sports.

So what did he do next? Instead of disappearing from sight, Sonnen went back to the playbook that made him famous to begin with: he started talking, candidly and loudly, and telling the truth about his infractions.

"I wouldn't shy away from a topic, even if it's one that brought me shame," he told reporters, referring to his drug use. And his missteps, just like his trash talk, kept Sonnen in the public eye.

Even though he fell from grace, the fall was short-lived. Soon after Fox fired him, the retired fighter joined rival network ESPN as a commentator, a role just as high-profile and lucrative as the one he'd held before his own doping scandal. Incredibly, Chael landed at ESPN a few years before the UFC finally landed its long-coveted ESPN deal, marking their move from Fox Sports. This move launched Chael to the pinnacle of his career as MMA commentator and analyst.

"We know Chael has made some mistakes in the past," an ESPN exec noted when the hiring was announced. "He's been honest. He's been up-front about it. He has paid for the mistakes that he has made, and he's moving forward . . . The insights that he has on the sport and the ways he sees it, our fans are going to be so much better from watching him on the air."

The point is not to go out and offend people, even though Sonnen prided himself on being provocative. The point is, when something demands attention, people will study it, stare at it longer, and look at it in more detail. They will also talk about it, and as we know, repetition of your message is critical. And if you have something special to offer, which Chael did despite his flaws, decision makers will take notice and give you more opportunities. Chael Sonnen steered into his problems, admitted his wrongdoing, and is now more popular than ever. Sonnen, having never won an official world title in combat sports, has nonetheless found lasting success in other ways. He lives in Portland, where I live, and I have observed him as a fight analyst, father, husband, son, and giver. Despite his superstardom, he is known for helping others and for his tireless generosity in his mission to give back to the wrestling community that made him. Though he may not have a title belt, one could say Chael is a world champion at life.

Grabbing immediate attention means your audience will take a harder look. If something is authentic, no matter how imperfect, then others will, at the very least, notice it and be able to come to a conclusion about it. An audience will look longer and harder at a message that demands attention. Regardless of whether they're studying the good or the bad in it, they will notice the details.

A few years later, a young man from a working-class background in Dublin, Ireland, entered the UFC in a hailstorm of publicity. In just a few short years, Conor McGregor went from living on social welfare to being worth well over $100 million. He became the most successful and wealthiest MMA fighter in history, shattering every pay-per-view record the UFC ever had while becoming the promotion company's first world champion in two weight divisions. Conor has often been compared to Chael as being an even bigger, badder, and better trash-talker. Some say he has even eclipsed the verbal acrobatics of bigger-than-life superstar and humanitarian Ali. Conor may not have taken his career from Chael's playbook, but he had to notice, as a man struggling to make ends meet back in Dublin, that getting attention means opportunity and money.

In Chael Sonnen's case, even if people didn't like him personally, or were offended by his comments, when they scrutinized the man—the source of the message—they discovered that he was a far better athlete than he had previously been given credit for. Sonnen is an excellent example of how you can use iconic thinking to break from the paralysis of the diluted voice, stand out from the crowd, get noticed, and succeed.

THE WEAKNESS OF CHOICE

8

Technological progress has merely provided us with
more efficient means for going backwards.
—Aldous Huxley, *Ends and Means*

On the surface, we tend to think of the ability to have a choice as a good thing.
But just as the overflow of information leads to the diluted voice,
there comes a point at which an abundance of choice makes it
hard for those offering the choice to be seen, and for those who
are trying to decide on something to, well, choose. When faced
with too many choices, we start to feel paralyzed.

Renowned psychologist and social theory professor Barry
Schwartz, author of the extremely popular 2004 book *The Paradox of Choice*, talks about the often overwhelming and daunting
number of choices on a simple trip to the supermarket as well as
a trip to the doctor's office. Consider the last time you went food
shopping. Throughout the 2000s the average American supermarket has had up to fifty thousand unique items on its shelves.
There are different options available for nearly every product we

ITEMS IN THE AVERAGE AMERICAN SUPERMARKET

1975	TODAY
8,948	47,211

Source: Consumer Reports, March 2014.

could want to buy. That means we spend more time, energy, and emotion figuring out what we want.

And maybe you don't think a few extra minutes in the supermarket are such a big deal. But these decision-making moments add up. The time we spend deliberating before making a choice is time taken away from focusing on anything else—work, creative endeavors, or interpersonal relationships—further diluting our important *connections* as individuals. All this time choosing forces our focus to the surface. We have so much to sort through, like with the online-dating vending machine, it's hard to look at anything deeply and not just take a purely superficial view.

Over the years, research has shown us some fascinating, and troubling, things about making choices. There is a much-talked-about and often-quoted study about decision making that is structured around choosing jam in one of these over-filled supermarkets. In his book, Schwartz shares the famous study about jam choices. A pair of experts in the field of choice, Sheena Iyengar of Columbia University and Mark Lepper of Stanford University—who have published academic papers and books like *The Art of Choosing, How Much Choice Is Too Much?*, *Choice and Its Consequences*, and *When Choice Is Demotivating*—did an interesting experiment. Iyengar and Lepper set up grocery store booths for shoppers to sample different flavors of jam. Subjects were presented with either twenty-four flavors or six flavors to try. They found that their subjects were *ten times more likely to actually buy* some of the jam if they were presented with a smaller number of varieties to taste.

Even though more people stopped to sample the selection of twenty-four jams, when it came time to buy, jam tasters couldn't make up their minds and wound up not making a purchase. There were simply too many choices to narrow their focus. With far fewer options, people felt confident and at ease in their selections, so they bought more jam. In this clear and convincing experiment, Iyengar and Lepper definitively showed that offering less creates more interaction and decision. The more consolidated something is, the easier it is to engage with and the more it creates demand. People may think they want more choices, but in reality they positively respond to less.

Less is just easier to process.

LESS IS MORE

JAM FLAVORS AVAILABLE	SHOPPERS WHO SAMPLED	SHOPPERS WHO PURCHASED
24	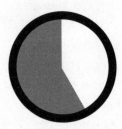	
6	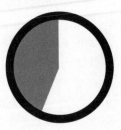	

In his catalytic book *Blink* (which helped create a whole new category of books with big ideas that help us), Malcolm Gladwell briefly discusses the Iyengar and Lepper jam study, saying, "Thirty percent of those who stopped by the six-choice booth ended up buying some jam, while only 3 *percent* of those who stopped by the bigger booth bought anything. Why is that? Because buying jam is a snap decision. You say to yourself, instinctively, I want that one. And if you are given too many choices, if you are forced to consider much more than your unconscious is comfortable with, you get paralyzed." And that's even with a decision as low stakes as choosing a jam flavor.

Limited options foster emotional positivity and more immediate connection—the opportunity to make an easy decision results in more engagement and more action. Iyengar and Lepper's results aren't an isolated case. Research across a range of products shows a similar result—decrease your offerings, increase your sales.

In a 2010 *New York Times* article, Alina Tugend discusses choice and information overload through the famous jam study as well as various others that focused on 401(k) plans and health decisions. She reflects on how some of these choices make us feel like we are being oversold, bringing up her own overwhelming experience just looking for something as basic as an internet service provider. "Companies were less interested in my welfare than in getting my money—and I didn't want to be a sucker." Overloading someone with too much choice makes them feel pressed and manipulated, rather than understood.

In the Consumers Union report (the advocacy, policy, and action arm of Consumer Reports), an intensive study was done on the presentation of health care options to consumers, from private insurance to Medicare. The Consumers Union report proves not only increased engagement from less choice but also much higher participation rates in health care and 401(k) programs by employees when they were offered fewer options.

When you reduce the number of consumer options (some choice is good), more people sign up. Offering less choice is not just a way to grow your audience but also, as seen in its ability to increase participation in health care coverage, in many ways can be used as a means of social improvement.

Presenting monolithic simplicities in health care could ultimately be the difference between life and death if it means that more people are covered. You see, from jam to insurance coverage, we are more likely to engage and not defer decisions if we just have limited, simpler choices. This is the simple supply-and-demand curve we all learned in Economics 101. Less of something means more value. Too much of something means less value.

It's counterintuitive, but people don't really want unlimited choices because "too much of everything" has turned making a choice into a painful undertaking.

Just why is it that making choices can be so paralyzing? Freud had a hypothesis called *ego depletion* that claimed our ego is innately linked to mental activities involving the transfer of energy. Social psychologist Roy F. Baumeister, in tribute to Freud's theory, demonstrated through his experiments that mental energy for exerting self-control is a limited, finite resource. Then, under Baumeister, postdoctoral student Jean Twenge, having firsthand experience of the exhaustion of her own wedding planning, began conducting a series of studies focused on *decision fatigue*. Those who had already made a number of choices on any given day—compared to those who had not had to deal with as many choices that day—had far less willpower and self-control. The abundance of choices and decision making had moved the test group along what psychologists call the Rubicon model of action phases to a point of weakness and apathy.

What's even more profound, as Schwartz argues, too much choice—leading with too much messaging or too many options—can have serious psychological repercussions.

According to Schwartz, choice overload creates

1. **anxiety** and **stress** about choosing and making the right choice
2. **paralysis**, or not making any choice at all, because one does not want to make the wrong choice
3. **dissatisfaction** with any choice made, wondering whether we could have made a different or better choice
4. **self-blame** for making a poor choice

In his TED Talk, Schwartz ventures that choice overload is one contributor to the soaring rates of clinical depression and suicide in the industrial world; after making a decision, "people have experiences that are disappointing because their standards are so high, and then, when they have to explain these experiences to themselves, they think they're at fault." The "opportunity cost" of so much choice is that when we do make a choice, we are ultimately dissatisfied with the choices we have made because we wonder if we made the right choice or could have chosen better.

For instance, take again our hypothetical walk down the breakfast cereal aisle of any grocery store. There you'll see a staggering example of just how many versions of not just breakfast cereal but a horde of similar items are now available to us. This can make choosing what you want frustrating and anxiety inducing.

Similarly, the feeling and psychological toll of *dilution* can have nearly identical and devastating consequences. *Anxiety* about whether one will ever be seen or heard, *stress* about not ever being seen or heard, *paralysis* caused by an internal feeling that we may not ever be seen or heard—so why even try?—are all real experiences that come from feeling "diluted." *Depression* from not having been seen or heard and ultimately *dissatisfaction* with our lives, because we feel invisible or that we will not be able to get our message out there, be recognized, and self-actualize.

These feelings could cause anyone of any economic class to engage in harmful behavior. When we have no hope or certainty about future expression, we might engage in behaviors that indicate that we don't care about the future. So, for many, dilution means pain.

Most of us inherently know we are fading into the background of an information-, services-, and consumer product–flooded world. The decision and choice fatigue that affects all of us, whether we are aware of it or not, is well documented. The *New York Times*, in 2011, published a fascinating article on social psychology studies across diverse personal decisions, from buying a car to choosing soap. In every instance it became obvious that the greater the number of choices we present to others, the less engaged they become over time. We have become grossly choice fatigued. We are more likely than ever to just disconnect rather than engage with anything that is too busy or gives us too many options.

Surplus of choice is directly related to the dilution effect—it again waters you down as an individual and mutes your impact on the world. The influx of thousands of new products and services combines with information overload to drown you and your product out. Like with the onslaught of mass information, explored in chapter one, this **abundance of choices that compete for attention around you is absolutely overwhelming.**

Technology has increased not just the amount of advertising we're exposed to but also the sheer volume of every kind of choice hammering us. Consider the absolutely mind-numbing volume of choices we have if we want to sit down and watch something on demand. Forget what to watch—first you have to decide whether to open Hulu, Netflix, DirecTV, Sling TV, Amazon, Roku, PlayStation . . . You get it. Whether we're shopping in a grocery store or browsing the web, we are faced with an overwhelming number of options—too many for any one person to digest. It makes your own voice, your own art, your own business, and your own life smaller and harder for others to see.

For an Iconist, there is a great lesson here: Yes, you are competing against an enormous amount of other content or products or people for attention. Blocks are the antidote. Blocks bring to light the things we need to see, in a way that they can be seen. By presenting your work through Blocks, you can help alleviate your audience's decision fatigue by being the clear, uncomplicated, obvious choice. Your Block will be a breath of fresh air.

PART TWO

TOY BLOCKS

9

There may be dice, and playthings, with letters on
them to teach children the alphabet by playing.
—John Locke, *Some Thoughts Concerning Education*

Whether we had a good childhood or a bad childhood, most of us would agree
that there was a kind of simplicity to our existence back then.
As we get older, life seems to get more and more complicated.
Taxes, jobs, girlfriends, boyfriends, wives, husbands, bosses,
car payments, mortgages, deadlines, house repairs, car repairs,
insurance, credit cards, checking accounts, work computers,
home computers, social networks . . .

In childhood, we don't have to deal with so much, well,
stuff. As children, we were easily transfixed by any unduly large
object that crossed our paths. Through personal and professional experience, time and time again, I have observed that
adults tend to respond the same way, even as our society throws
more complicated things at us. Interestingly, we still—often
subconsciously—gravitate toward simpler objects and situ-
ations. (Think back to the famous jam study.) This is true for
large objects, and it is true for any big, massive thing. Whether
it is a powerfully imposing feature like the Grand Canyon or a

hulking piece of heavy construction equipment, people tend to be transfixed by anything that is exceedingly large in relation to the environment around it.

By understanding and using the same principles that capture children's attention, we can improve the way we deliver information to *anyone*, of *any age*.

John Locke, one of the greatest Enlightenment thinkers, is the guy who said all human beings are born with a tabula rasa (blank slate) and what children eventually become is purely determined by their environment.

Whether or not you believe in the "blank slate" idea, Locke's ideas about learning will be very important to us here.

For a toddler, new styles of toys, dolls, cars, and stuffed animals come and go, but one learning toy that has remained constant and virtually unchanged in popular culture for more than three hundred years is the ABC block. These blocks were originally developed in seventeenth-century England. They impressed Locke, whose work focused on understanding human development. Locke hailed "dice and playthings" as a breakthrough for early literacy, declaring that using these ABC toy blocks was the most enjoyable way to instill an interest in letters. With toy blocks, he argued, children could learn to read "without perceiving it to be anything but a sport."

When we are children, it's normal for us to learn in straightforward, structured, *Sesame Street*–like ways. Whether it's a TV show or picture books, we learn by looking at big, bold, often repetitive images that present numbers or problems in a strong, visually simplified way. Counting to ten can take over a minute with a purple Count von Count Muppet taunting you from the screen, especially when the single digits take up the entire television. Elementary school math books use practical and obvious examples like an actual giant pie (Block) to illustrate fractions.

Nearly all children's storybooks and elementary workbooks are designed this way. But we can learn through these techniques throughout our entire lives. (Arguably, part of the nostalgia we feel for childhood and shows like *Sesame Street* stems from the *primal comfort* of learning through these simple, obvious methods. We're profoundly comforted when at least one thing makes instant, apparent sense, and that's exactly what happens when we're presented with things we can quickly and easily latch on to.)

Environment has obvious effects on human development, and simple, oversized shapes tend to imprint on the developing brains of babies and toddlers. As Haig Kouyoumdjian writes in *Psychology Today*, the portion of our human brains dedicated to image processing is multiples larger than the small part dedicated to language or word processing. So, in a world of overcomplicated communication, large objects can have an even more profound impact on adults trying to learn or take anything in. In a study published in the *Journal of Experimental Education*, two populations of students were shown text with and without visual displays on the subjects of geography and science. It was shown consistently in both groups that those who studied text with visual displays had a proven higher rate of memory and knowledge acquisition. In short, no matter who we are, imagery just helps us to learn and retain more.

As a society, we make a monumental mistake when we stop delivering information in elementary ways as people grow older. *The true revelation of Blocks is that humans of every age really do overwhelmingly prefer to take in information and learn through the same big, bold imagery that we craved as kids.* A 1984 article published in *Instructional Science* showed that visual supplements become *more* important with more complex information—in other words, the more complicated something is, the more a visual element like a Block provides a needed access point to learning it.

I decided to call Blocks "Blocks" because of the mesmerizing quality a toy block has to a toddler. Any monolithic thing that can be instantly perceived, with any sort of intricacy inside it, demands our attention like a warning label or a stop sign.

Blocks work because at a primal level we find comfort and pleasure in large, uncomplicated objects.

As with any children's elementary school workbook, when sophisticated information is connected to a huge, elephantine image or statement, a remarkable thing also occurs in the adult mind: we're soothed and comforted by the image. Its size, clear

form, and instant perceivability communicate to us that, no matter how difficult the information attached to it may be, we can relate it to this immense, oversized, simple thing. In my experience of consulting and giving public talks to students and clients, I can observe from the stage or the front of the classroom slight smiles and looks of contentment once I fire up my slides. This is true even when the slides are dry and boring. I see a look of calm wash over the audience the second I start talking about ideas while supporting them with a visual image of any kind. This connection—the oversized monolithic object being a sort of anchor in complex and intricate information—is the key to why and how Blocks work.

The soul never thinks without a mental picture.
—Aristotle

As you start thinking and communicating like an Iconist, you'll see that massive, oversized Blocks make any collection of specific or intricate information more readily digestible. Large Blocks give people something they can instantly grab on to. Include with your Block the more complex information you are trying to get across, and people will not only be compelled to stop and look; they will be magnetized and genuinely intrigued. It is a reflexive mechanism of human perception. There is true power in any simple Block that has an intricacy within it or coming right behind it—as we'll see in the coming chapters. Like the letters and images on the simple toy block, detail and intricacy within a simple and accessible form are mesmerizing to us.

The idea that massive things not only attract but can soothe young children is easily observable by the existence of tens of thousands of videos streaming on the internet. These videos have names like "Dumpers and Diggers" and "Mighty Machines" and are extremely simple. They have no effects, music, or narration and are basically just footage of heavy machinery and trucks doing what they are meant to do—moving dirt, digging giant holes, moving scrap, dumping sand, and basically carrying on their industrial tasks, repetitively. What is amazing about these unpolished videos is how they can hold the attention of children for hours . . . and not just children, it turns out. All of us can be immediately hooked and captivated.

As Daymond John, celebrity entrepreneur, investor, and FUBU fashion label founder, shared on *Shark Tank*, "Last year I was walking around the beach in Miami; they were doing construction. They were moving the sand—and I found that I stood there, looking at that construction, for about three hours. I was fascinated by it."

The point is, there is just something transfixing and calming to us all, regardless of age, about a massive thing doing a simple, immediately understood task. Through my work and observation I see time and again that when anything complex facing adults is brought to them and presented up front in a Block, simple, "marqueed" way (communicated in an overly large, banner-like style, like the massive lettered marquee sign above the entrance of any Broadway theater), the same tranquil mesmerism attracts and relaxes them, and they are able to process and lean in to what is being offered up.

When connected to a Block, anything and everything becomes remarkably easier and pleasing to perceive. As we get older and more distracted in an overbusy world, we need these Blocks to be bigger, brighter, and bolder—and to be delivered with the same intent that we use to attract a baby's attention.

Anyone communicating in any medium must consciously and deliberately lead with a big, bold, simple Block as the first point of contact if they want to be seen.

Yet somewhere along the way we got caught up in the swamp of all that we know, wanting to show the world just how intricate, complex, and profound our thoughts and talents are. This tendency has only served to obscure all that we want others to see. Blocks bring us back to the innate, prewired circuit board we were all born with to distinguish what really matters.

We've all heard the old cliché that someone "couldn't see the forest for the trees." But the problem is that today, too often, we're bombarded with so much information that we can't pick out the individual trees in a forest of messaging. Trees are monolithic and iconic, easy to perceive—entire forests are not. Blocks let us take a breather. They give us something big and solid to grab on to in a sea of white noise.

So if everyone's looking for a tree in the forest, why not just give them one? If you're going to be part of the solution to messaging overload, you'll need to face just how insanely loud your audience's environment already is—as we explored in part one of this book.

We live in a climate where your Blocks can serve as mind food for a starving populace. In other words, when there's a firehose of things jetting at us, we need something big and solid to grab on to even more.

But where should you start? In the next few chapters, we'll look at examples of successful Blocks in various forms—from the structures around us to the arts to communications.

In reality, Blocks exist everywhere and you are already using them on some level. You just don't know that you are using them, so you aren't likely to be using them effectively or consistently.

Blocks are a way to signal the traffic of like minds toward like minds. They should never be viewed as a method to alter or change who you are but rather as a system to help you determine what should be highlighted as your primary representation of self. When you understand the anatomy of Blocks in your particular field, you will be able to craft simple, visible Blocks that represent you. Repeat your Block everywhere and you will demand your audience stop, take notice, and latch on.

THE LAWS OF GRAVITY 10

Gravity wins over all other known forces.
—**Andrea M. Ghez**

From the earliest moments in history, humankind has looked to nature as a definition of perfection. From the beginning, we've strived to mimic what seems to work effortlessly in the natural world. Ancient leaders needed a way to captivate and draw the attention of people to pull them into a common cause. People have always been attracted to the simple, massive forms of the sun and the moon.

In the ancient world, symmetry was far more profound. True symmetry occurred only in nature, not in man-made objects. One could even see the Great Pyramids at Giza as an attempt to replicate these powerful prehistoric forms. We carry this yearning for balance within us innately and instinctively to this day.

When ancient people sought perfection, they looked toward the one monolithic shape that was ever present in their lives. In the heavens hung the most perfect object in nature: the sun. We've been drawn to that symmetrical ideal ever since, and we strive for it in our earthly creations. It's why we crave huge, bold objects—and simple, bold ideas. It's why we're hardwired to connect with simple blocks of information and to filter out anything that's not massive, clear, and repetitively consistent like the rising and the setting of the sun.

Mountains have a similar power to captivate our attention. But why?

Imagine you're part of one of the first civilizations—a people who developed the first languages and built some of the first free-standing structures. Where did your quest for understanding begin? Where did your knowledge come from? What were you trying to emulate? That which you saw already perfect and working in the world around you.

Mountain peaks collect snow, which eventually turns to snowmelt, creating tributaries and streams that feed rivers. Water is the requisite for life; rivers mean game for hunting and fish for catching. Their waters feed alpine forests, which provide wood for shelter and fire for cooking. We can't see a river from fifty miles away, but we can see a mountain in the distance, and for over a hundred miles there is something that gives us instant comfort upon seeing its imposing image.

Throughout our existence, mountains have represented a source of life for all kinds of land-dwelling species. We tend to see them in terms of natural beauty, but it is impossible to separate our concept of beauty from what is good and helpful to us.

Mountain monolith = TRIANGLE = shelter and food
Sun monolith = CIRCLE = energy, warmth, and vegetation
Lake monolith = CIRCLE or OVAL =
refreshment, relief, and life

Mountains mean fortification and protection from the elements. Mountains represent the tools to protect us from predators. They mean sanctuary and refuge from enemies. These massive Blocks of earth are literally a symbol of life.

It makes sense, then, that our attraction to Blocks is linked to our concept of physical beauty. It is likely the large size and simple forms of objects in the natural world, like mountains and the sun, that explains our attraction to Block imagery. Like mountains, Blocks are symbols that reflexively freeze our eye.

Simple and easily recognizable shapes and forms are everywhere. If I asked you to walk around your neighborhood and count every geometric shape your eyes alighted on before you go home, it would take you a week. Blocks are like these shapes—they can exist all around you, responsible for all the recognizable images in your day without you being consciously aware of their effect on you.

Elementary geometric shapes are the building Blocks of all architecture. Doors are rectangles (so are bricks), arches are half circles, and so on. Yet we don't think we are driving around in a bunch of "geometry" every day unless it's pointed out. Blocks are the same—once you understand Blocks you will see them everywhere and all around you. The simplest visual Blocks are often symmetrical in form or nature. The word *symmetry* is derived from the Greek σύμμετρος, *symmetros*, which means "well balanced." It can be defined as something that's completely proportional, or just pleasing to the eye. In other words, *simple, balanced shapes are even more naturally magnetic.*

Mario Livio, a senior astrophysicist at the Space Telescope Science Institute, wrote a book on the subject of symmetry in which he argues that our brains latch on to symmetry because it is so common—all around us in nature and all across the universe. Studies in biology have also shown that humans and animals are naturally attracted to symmetry because symmetry is an indication of genetic and physical health.

SYMMETRICAL
PLEASING TO THE EYE

NOT SYMMETRICAL
NOT PLEASING TO THE EYE

It is how we measure beauty in Western society. This natural, instinctual attraction to the beautiful or symmetrical is the exact same mechanism that make Blocks effective.

There's also an opposing concept in sociology called perceptual bias. It argues that our perception of beauty and human attraction is rooted in the fact that the brain processes symmetrical imagery much faster than asymmetrical imagery. We are attracted to those things that we can most easily process. Add to that making them big and bold, and it makes almost anything arresting.

Like gravity, the force behind what causes Icons and Blocks to operate works for the same reasons, and is seemingly as timeless. Gravity worked the same way five thousand years ago as it does today; it worked long before Newton ever discovered it and gave it a name.

Blocks and Icons are scalable. When I say that, I'm saying that a small child perceives and remembers the shape of a small, square block for the same reason that an adult easily remembers the triangular shape of a massive Egyptian pyramid. Icons work no matter the scale—a toy block is thousands of times smaller than an Egyptian pyramid, yet forms that are simple in shape stand out and enter the mind much more easily.

Simplicity of form, as well as the size of an object, is at work here.

Blocks are everywhere, all around you and out there in the world. They are based on simple observations, but once you understand how they work, you can see them as not only what attracts us iconically but, on a microlevel, the building Blocks of nearly all human construction.

The shape and boldness of a thing are what we notice first. They make a thing easiest for us to grasp. Most advertisers and messengers think they do this—they don't. They water down or overcomplicate imagery and their message to the extent that it becomes pointless or even cheesy, failing to stand out and connect.

Blocks—the elephantine, effortless forms we've examined in such detail—bypass our resistance to microinformation, leaving powerful, instant impressions. Based on the same principles, simplicity of form pervades our resistance to information overload. As you continue through *The Iconist*, you will learn simple techniques that allow you to distill your ideas down to the most fundamental of constructs, at least on the surface, so that more complicated communication will remain, resonate, and endure with the audience that you wish to receive it.

The Blocks that you create will work, according to the same set of rules, over the span of ten seconds, ten minutes, or ten thousand years. Repeat the Block boldly, tirelessly, and you'll have "Icon'd" it. Icons have a universal and magical gravitational pull on our attention regardless of age or size.

Repetition of the right Block in any medium will generate a bull's-eye of primal demand to your desired audience. Like gravity, Blocks grab attention, and with repetition they quickly become Icons of the mind.

THE MONOLITH

11

Simplicity is the ultimate sophistication.
—**William Gaddis,** *The Recognitions*

In 1949 an architect in his late forties—a man with a messy personal life—was fading into obscurity. His banal and unextraordinary work included a series of housing projects in his hometown of Philadelphia. But in 1950, as an architect in residence at the American Academy in Rome, this man, far past his prime, decided to tour the ancient ruins of the world. Starting in Rome with sights like the Colosseum, he went on to explore the wonders of the world in Egypt and Greece. In what should have been the winter of his career, Louis Kahn transformed himself into what many consider to be the most influential American architect of the twentieth century. Kahn's work would eventually show how Blocks hold the same undeniable force as gravity. They capture attention and do not let us go or give us a choice.

In 2003 Nathaniel Kahn, Louis Kahn's son from one of three separate families—which he kept secret, supporting each individually—made a film about his quest to learn more about his mysterious, masterful father, today recognized as a towering figure in the annals of architecture. (*My Architect: A Son's Journey* would go on to receive universal acclaim and was nominated for the Academy Award for Documentary Feature.) While some of the greatest architects of the century would eventually hail him as a genius, back in 1950, the still-unextraordinary Louis Kahn found himself packing off to Rome after the birth of another child under scandalous circumstances. Though he was almost fifty years old, it was this trip to Rome that altered the course of his life's work. Kahn's encounter of the Colosseum likely led him to tour more of the world's wonders.

Kahn's tour of these ancient wonders directed him toward a distinct and deeply personal style—a profound marriage of the complex and the monolithic. Mirroring aspects of the ancient ruins he visited, he worked with simple geometric shapes on a massive scale, but his structures revealed a staggering amount of complexity when the viewer came closer to them or stepped inside.

In his film, Nathaniel Kahn interviews modern master architect I. M. Pei. He asks Pei why he considers Louis Kahn to be the greatest of his time, especially considering that Pei himself had been so prolific, designing dozens and dozens of buildings across the globe, while Kahn only created seven significant buildings in his post-wonders rebirth.

Pei responded, "Three or four masterpieces [are] more important than 50 [or] 60 buildings . . . architecture has to have the quality of time." In other words, it's about quality, not quantity.

Throughout history, the Egyptian pyramids have been held as one of the great wonders of the physical world. The fact that the pyramids are literally wondrous helps; they are an engineering feat, constructed with limited technology, and how exactly the huge blocks of stone were hauled into place remains somewhat of a mystery. However, their simplicity is far more important than their wonder when it comes to why they stand out and endure in our collective consciousness.

These structures are an excellent example of how Blocks (simple large shapes) can become Icons, a touchstone held in our collective minds. An examination of all the Seven Wonders of the World is a remarkable way to illustrate this.

Interestingly, it is almost impossible to get any type of expert to agree on what the "Seven Wonders" actually are. Here are some of the more common and obvious contenders: the Great Pyramids of Egypt, Stonehenge, the mammoth Moai heads of Easter Island, Machu Picchu, the Taj Mahal, the Colosseum, the Colossus of Rhodes, the Hanging Gardens of Babylon, the Mayan ruins at Chichen Itza, the Statue of Zeus at Olympia, the Temple of Artemis, the Great Wall of China, and the Tomb of Mausolus. For anyone who wasn't counting, that's thirteen contenders for the list of seven, and there are more.

Go online and you will find many more lists and "scientific experts" staking claims or having disagreements as to what the "real" Seven Wonders are. It seems laymen and scientists all have their own ideas as to what truly makes something "wondrous."

One appealing solution to the argument has been to put the Seven Wonders in subcategories such as the Seven Natural Wonders, the Seven Ancient Wonders, the Seven Medieval Wonders, or even the New Seven Wonders. *USA Today* and *Good Morning America* coined that last list in 2006 after redefining what we might consider truly "wondrous." It even included the readers' choice of an "eighth wonder," the Grand Canyon.

USA TODAY'S NEW SEVEN WONDERS OF THE WORLD

1 **POTALA PALACE** — **LHASA** TIBET, CHINA

2 **OLD CITY OF JERUSALEM** — **JERUSALEM** ISRAEL

3 **POLAR ICE CAPS** — **POLAR REGIONS**

4 **PAPAHANAU-MOKUAKEA** — **HAWAII** USA

5 **THE INTERNET** — **EARTH** MILKY WAY

6 **MAYAN RUINS** — **YUCATAN** THE AMERICAS

7 **GREAT MIGRATION** — **TANZANIA & KENYA**

8 **GRAND CANYON** — **ARIZONA** USA

There may be a few places on the *USA Today* list that you have never even heard of; it was developed by a group of scientists and cultural observers from various fields. The panel included experts like marine biologist Sylvia Earl, theologian Bruce Feiler, international travel writer and novelist Pico Iyer, global explorer Holly Morris, high-altitude archaeologist John Reinhard, and astrophysicist Neil deGrasse Tyson.

Most, if not all, of the examples in the *USA Today* New Wonders list do not resonate with the average person in terms of what they collectively understand to be the Seven Wonders (except for the readers' choice of the Grand Canyon). The Hanging Gardens of Babylon don't exist anymore, and the internet and the Great Migration in the Serengeti are somewhat intangible in terms of a visual image or picture in the mind.

The Seven Wonders of the average woman or man on the street—the pop culture list—are a simple and fair-minded, if not definitive, list:

The **Great Pyramids** are immense △ **triangles.**

The **Colosseum** is a massive ○ **circle.**

Stonehenge is a display of giant ▯ **rectangles** or a huge ○ **circle,** if you happen to be the aliens that built them. 😌

The **Great Wall** is a series of colossal interlocked ▯ **rectangles** and ☐ **squares.**

The **Moai heads of Easter Island** are enormous ▯ **rectangles** with ☺ faces carved into them.

The **Taj Mahal** is a gigantic ☐ **rectangle** with a ◯ **circle** on top of it.

And the **Grand Canyon** is simply **HUGE** and visually extreme in its gargantuan contrast to the environment surrounding it.

Give any man or woman on the street an impromptu quiz, and he or she would likely name items from this same list of wonders—and only one of the experts' seven.

The question is, *Why does the "expert list" vary so widely from the generally understood Seven Wonders within our pop culture?* Well, these experts are likely more concerned with the literal concept of the greatness of something and are less likely to be taken in by a surface notion, which is exactly the point. It is the wonders with simple shapes on the surface that we most *remember*. This simple surface notion makes them *endure* in our minds—in short, it is what makes them iconic.

The common denominator of the pop culture list has more to do with these wonders' simplicity, not the degree of awe they inspire. Each wonder's design can be easily distilled into a basic shape. Of them all, the Taj Mahal has the most complicated structure, and it is essentially just a rectangle with a circle on it.

Iconic wonders endure because they are physical, visual Blocks—their basic form readily gives us a clear image that endures in our brains. So even though many of the new wonders put forth by experts may be much more incredible in their intricacy of design, scale, or cultural significance, the primal brain in us all will latch on to and instantly recall the Icon or Block. We associate a tremendous amount of knowledge with these images, but it's the simple shape that first tends to come to mind.

TAJ

PYRAMID

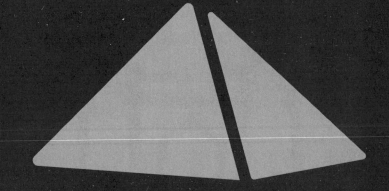

COLOSSEUM

MOAI

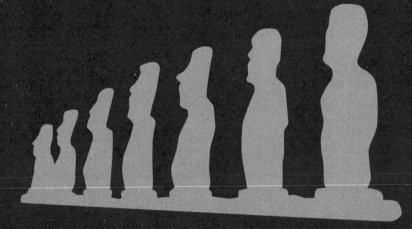

STONE

GREAT

GRAND

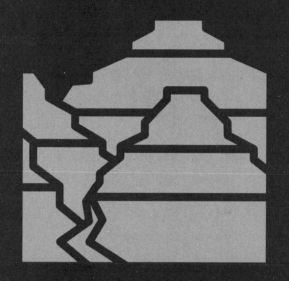

Machu Picchu and the Tomb of Mausolus are astoundingly wondrous, and yet much more complicated than the sights in the pop culture list of the Seven Wonders, which are clearly monolithic Blocks—and now Icons. It is this complexity, despite their merit, that makes them less memorable to us.

It is simplicity of form, the Block, not beauty or age, that causes these pop-cultural wonders to sit so clearly within our minds.

Just as we wonder at these ancient ruins today, populations of the future will likely hail Kahn's structures as special. Master architect Clive Wilkinson was a protégé of the legendary Frank Gehry and served as project manager on Gehry's exalted masterpiece Walt Disney Concert Hall in downtown Los Angeles. Wilkinson has been listed on *Fast Company*'s 100 Most Creative People and is the architect and designer behind the astonishing Googleplex in Mountain View, California. He is known as a pioneer in modern workplace design. Clive calls Kahn "a master of primal geometry" and says that "part of the seduction is the elemental simplicity of his work."

His designs put Blocks into practice, echoing the composition of ancient ruins and playing off of the magnetic interplay between the intricate and the elephantine. This can easily be seen in his opus, the National Assembly Building of Bangladesh in the country's capital, Dhaka. It may be the greatest single piece of architecture of the twentieth century, and one Kahn never beheld in its tangible entirety because it was not completed until almost a decade after his death.

What makes the building so astonishing, aside from the fact that it is located in one of the poorest countries in the world, is how it sits inside a water base along grass fields as a geometric,

LOUIS KAHN

elegant monolith of a structure. It is a profound and simple geometric cathedral of architecture whose immense size exerts a gravitational pull on the eye. What is even more remarkable is the complexity of detail once you get up close and go inside. As daylight moves across the painted patina of the interior walls, smaller geometric stone cutouts within the walls and the symmetrically designed metal grating are illuminated—the intricacy and detailing of a work of art. This piece of architecture would not have this much power without the detail. The exquisite detail would not be as profound without the massive Block shell. This is the power of the symbiotic relationship that exists between the immense and the intricate. They feed each other and need each other for the other to have power. This is the primordial truth and nature of Blocks.

For an Iconist, the Seven Wonders and Kahn's architecture offer an intriguing lens through which to view your work.

Of course, visual art, music, ideas, and products are very different from the monolithic structures we've explored here . . . but by emulating these structures' simplicity of form and thinking about what makes them endure, we can help our work to draw just as much of a gravitational force on any audience.

VIOLENT TIMES

Blocks in Visual Art

A work of art must carry in itself its complete
significance and impose it upon the beholder even
before he can identify the subject matter.
—**Henri Matisse,** *Notes of a Painter*

Blocks are built into substantial, memorable Icons in any medium—it just takes repetition to do so.

All art, graphic design, and visual imagery grabs attention according to this primal law. Central imagery is the Block that immediately captures attention and holds it, imprinting any visual piece on the mind. It is the reason Manet and Gauguin, regardless of their talent, are not nearly as known or recognized as their contemporary Van Gogh. It's the reason many of us immediately recognize the works of Andy Warhol. And it's what lies behind the seemingly overnight success of modern fine artist and photographer Melanie Pullen.

In the mid-2000s, Melanie exploded out of obscurity to become a hugely collected and influential photographer. Melanie's first show, *High Fashion Crime Scenes*, held at the Ace Gallery in Beverly Hills, resulted in international acclaim: a documentary, a book, a slew of popular press, and her work being coveted by the world's most prominent and influential collectors. In 2018 Melanie's work was invited into the exalted Getty Museum in Los Angeles as part of the exhibit *Icons of Style: A Century of Fashion Photography, 1911–2011*. She was one of the only living artists whose work was selected to be in the exhibition and one of her pieces has been added to the Getty's permanent collection.

Melanie Pullen happens to be my childhood friend from the belly of L.A. (we go back long enough for me to know her father has long been a professional pool shark—his compatriots call him "Wayne the Train"). But our friendship has nothing to do with the reason I'm telling you about her.

What's so fascinating is that Melanie had not been a working photographer before this meteoric success. Her work is based off cinematic recreations of 1930s murder scenes remade with high-fashion models and couture clothing. Inspired by LAPD and NYPD crime scene files, photo after photo shows beautiful women floating in midair, or a femme fatale splayed out lifelessly on the cold marble of a Metro station or abandoned along a pier. Each is a dark and beautiful setting filled with a model convincingly feigning death. You instantly understand each image in a fraction of a second. It wasn't the clothes, or the salacious subject matter, or the Gatsbyesque flair of her work that made the photos, or Melanie, famous. Pullen isn't after shock value: "An observer needs to see an image repeated in a similar form and style, at least three times, to get it," she explains. It was the Block that got her seen, and generated instant demand.

Elegant and gruesome at the same time, her work is also notable for its massive physical size—Pullen's prints usually range from four to ten feet in width. Why does she produce such large-format prints? "Because they are bold and have an impact on an audience," she says.

Her second solo show, *Violent Times*, became the largest still-photography show ever held in the history of the western United States. The show was too big for Ace Gallery, her Beverly Hills rep and one of the most prestigious galleries in Los Angeles. So this show was held in the 78,800-square-foot Desmond Building on Wilshire Boulevard, taking up the entire city block. The opening was mobbed by over two thousand people.

Melanie's work with *Violent Times* established her as one of the preeminent up-and-coming fine artists in the world. The massive show contained dozens of staggering cinematic images, some as much as eight feet high and twelve feet wide; the series is made up of four parts: *Battle Scenes*, *Soldier Portraits*, *The Combat Soldiers* (four of which appear on pages 112–117), and *Biochemical Warfare*. The series cemented her place as a darling of respected art collectors around the globe.

Acclaimed cinematographer Kramer Morgenthau, who directed photography on such films as *Creed II*, *Thor: The Dark World*, and *Terminator Genisys*, as well as dark and beautiful television shows like *Boardwalk Empire* and *Game of Thrones*, deeply admires Melanie, saying, "Her work is powerfully representational of the kind of iconic imagery you would see used in cinematography. Every one of her still photographs tells a story. Melanie is completely fearless. Her work has a confidence and strength. There is a boldness of color, of contrast and of content. It pops out of the frame and is uncompromising."

As Melanie learned, the repetition of messages, images, music, any form of art, or ideas builds over time into a monolithic message, made up of the smaller, similar parts. Of *Violent Times*, she says, "I dramatized the aesthetics of early portraiture and battle imagery, creating an extensive series that questions our perceptions and our ingrained desire to glamorize violence." If you are trying to communicate a complex message like that, the average person can only absorb one to three major concepts at a time. That is why it is so important to repeat yourself and stick with just a few points for minutes, hours, days, weeks, months, years, even decades. Simplicity of form and emotion speeds up the process and allows you to control it.

Melanie's work is expanding. She is now photographing magazine covers and directing theatrical, elaborately produced performances of her work. These live performances are living renderings of her haunting and beguiling photographs. Melanie's use of Blocks clearly worked to catapult her into prominence and generate demand for her work. As her presence grows beyond art photography, she has begun to influence popular culture.

Innovator and architect Clive Wilkinson praises Melanie's work. He explained to me, "Like [Louis] Kahn, her work, at its root, taps into the primal. As with iconic architecture, a painting or photograph has to first catch you, and invite you into it, as a portal. Then it has to lead you somewhere to engage. The complexity and story in her work holds you, and has to be dense so that you stay, to figure it out."

Melanie Pullen's seemingly straightforward, bold imagery exemplifies the interplay between the intricate and the monolithic. Whether in three-dimensional structures or visual images—the boldly simple, immediately perceivable grabs attention, leading us to the complexity behind or within it.

In order to succeed, a Block image must be grasped with near-total understanding in a microsecond. Before your brain can process it, you already know what it is on a primal level, giving you an anchor from which you can explore the creation's intrinsic complexity.

The speed at which something simple can move from the physical world into an enduring mental concept determines whether it will defeat all the other sensory information competing for attention. Complexity—the antithesis of Block construction—creates a delay in that transfer, and even a millisecond can be the difference between capturing or losing an audience for good. This is often the razor's edge between success and failure.

Vincent van Gogh's enduring iconic status proves the power of signature imagery, yet so many artists don't create work with instant recognizability and repetitive style. It is counterintuitive to what it means to be a "creative artist." Even so, many artists spend their lives working in a narrow creative box. I believe this is because somehow they intuitively know that signature style is what it takes to cut through. It may take an artist years to create that box, yet that is what an artist who wants to have mass appeal will do.

Not everything is meant to have mass appeal; there's room (and a need!) for variation and subtlety at times. But by understanding Blocks we can decide what we want our signature style to be, or what we want to be known for, and make it a conscious choice.

Blocks are a tool that will help your work stand out. *The Iconist* is not a book to alter your work. It is about offering you a tool that you can use to garner attention—but only if attention is what you are after. Not all things should grab attention, but an appreciation of Blocks gives you the choice to do so if you want. Think of it like a certain type of paintbrush you might use, or the color red. You can use it to get the effect of attention you desire, or choose not to. I love obscure art that doesn't use Blocks. The point is that every artist should know what grabs attention and determine whether they are going to use the tool of Blocks *as their choice*. Most artists use Blocks unwittingly or not at all.

Van Gogh died before receiving recognition, but many of his pieces have since become iconic. Some of his most recognizable works like the *Sunflowers* series, *Bedroom in Arles*, *Café Terrace at Night*, *A Pair of Shoes*, *Bull*, and *Tree* follow the same primal Block: **a dominant central image**. Not all Van Gogh's paintings follow this pattern, of course, but these are the images that have endured in our popular concept of the man and his art. Each of these paintings has a giant popping central image filling up the center of its canvas like a yield sign. You instantly get it without having to think. Van Gogh was painting Blocks and it made his works become Icons. His place in art history and his enduring popularity is forever the proof.

Meanwhile, Gauguin, once a roommate of Van Gogh, painted magnificent scenes playing with light and bold color masterfully, yet his recognizability and fame in the world pales in comparison to the higher-contrast, instantly understood *oversized central imagery* of his counterpart. Paul Gauguin didn't regularly use Blocks. When Van Gogh was painting a field, an object, or a person, you instantly understand what it is—with many of Gauguin's works, it can take you a second. The extra split second it takes to perceive and take in any imagery makes all the difference. It is in a *moment* that you pull someone in to your art or lose them.

VAN GOGH

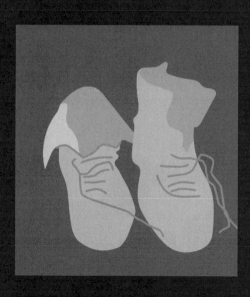

GAUGUIN

MARILYN

SOUP CAN

The instant understandability allows the work to permeate faster and more aggressively into the collective consciousness and for others to engage with your work with immediacy.

We can point to countless other artists whose enduring popularity, I'd argue, stems directly from their use of Block imagery. Take Andy Warhol with his *Campbell's Soup Cans*, *Marilyn Diptych*, *Cow Wallpaper*, *Mao Tse-Tung*, *Double Elvis*, self-portraits, and his endless array of pop masterpieces. Many don't realize that Warhol was also an illustrator of intricate, realistic imagery. It is likely his vast technical skills in fine art that powerfully informed his preference for simplicity.

The beloved painter Frida Kahlo's body of creative work is exceedingly varied. I admired many of her pieces firsthand at her house in Coyoacán, Mexico City. Across all the different subjects and styles among her two hundred paintings, drawings, and sketches, she has come to be known almost *purely* and iconically for her self-portraits. Though they make up only a fraction of her work, *these repetitive images*—that is, only her Block—have cut through to the global collective consciousness.

The most iconic artists, past and present, have always, at the very least, had an unwitting understanding of Blocks, and it is why they connect on a larger scale to others over time.

Let's look at it another way. In physics, Mass × Acceleration = Force. So, for Blocks, the mass is the Block. Its repetition acts as acceleration, and the combination of the two forces its way through the clutter cloud and into the mind of your intended recipient.

Blocks as a formula will give you confidence and calm you with the knowledge that you are leading with the correct

BLOCK×REPETITION= BREAKING THROUGH THE CLUTTER CLOUD

(MASS×ACCELERATION=FORCE)

simplicity and that you will be getting attention and will be understood. They also provide onlookers with the opportunity to relax, appreciate, and retain more of the complicated information you are throwing at them.

In all visual art and design the Block—a large, central, instantly recognizable image—works just like the immediacy of a stop sign.

When you have an instantly recognizable, big, bold, high-contrast, obvious image dominating the canvas, the boldness will draw us to look further into details and complexity within. This is what Blocks do. Bold, central imagery creates a jolt. That jolt demands attention. Craft it with beauty—or, in the case of a concept, an authentic understanding of your audience's primary emotional concern—and your message will stick. Blocks first magnetize (like bold, high-contrast warning labels), draw us in, and then, with the more intricate content within, mesmerize and imprint on the mind. When Blocks are repeated, Icons are born.

NURSERY RHYMES

Blocks in Music

Trusting your individual uniqueness
challenges you to lay yourself open.
—James **Broughton**

Emotion is obvious. If we feel emotion, we pay attention. This could be prompted by the melody of a song, a single word, a concept or an idea, an image, or anything else that triggers feelings, be they faint or extreme.

Ludwig van Beethoven was the reigning musical Iconist of his time, so much so that he was mocked by critics and contemporaries during and even after his life for the childlike quality of some of his melodies. In 1899, over one hundred years after "Ode to Joy" was written, the American music critic Philip Hale described what is now Beethoven's most revered composition thus: "But oh, the pages of stupid and hopelessly vulgar music! The unspeakable cheapness of the chief tune, '*Freude, Freude!*'" The very simplicity that Hale *hated* is the repetitive Block melody that causes the composition to not only stick but endure.

A few years earlier, on November 6, 1882, composer and music teacher Ferdinand Praeger published his case against repetition, "On the Fallacy of the Repetition of Parts in the Classical Form," in which he stated,

> All will readily admit that a first impression, however striking, is weakened when followed by an immediate repetition. Would ever a poet think of repeating half of his poem; a dramatist a whole act; a novelist a whole chapter? Such a proposition would be at once rejected as childish. Why should it be otherwise with music? . . . Since any whole part-repetition in poetry would be rejected as childish, or as the emanation of a disordered brain, why should it be otherwise with music?

Despite the criticism, Beethoven's instinctual use of Blocks is what brought listeners into the vast complexity of his compositions, and still does over two hundred years later. The four-note opening of his Fifth Symphony (that instantly recognizable *dun–dun–da–dun!*) also works as a melodic Block. The symphonies are intricate, but the Block melodies are the nursery rhyme–like access points that allow us to embrace them. It is precisely what Hale reviles as *hopelessly vulgar* that is hailed as one of the most beautiful compositions ever written. Beethoven was one of the most accomplished musicians of his time. With Blocks, we can understand and focus on the relationship between complexity and simplicity as the simple mechanism that it is.

In music, the Block is a leading DOMINANT REPETITIVE melody, lyric, or rhythm that will immediately and irrepressibly force itself into the mind of a listener. It's what grabs our attention and pulls us into a song. It is the Block that immediately gets us to stop and listen. Blocks are the reason we can't get a song

out of our heads. They create the "hook"—that is what makes a song "catchy." Blocks capture our attention and do not let go.

Elizabeth Margulis, music perception and cognition expert and author of *On Repeat: How Music Plays the Mind*, conducted a clever experiment through her research at the Music Cognition Lab at the University of Arkansas where she found conclusive evidence for the power of repetition in music, which she presents in a study titled "Aesthetic Responses to Repetition in Unfamiliar Music." Using the characteristically dissonant and overtly nonrepetitive compositions of twentieth-century composer Elliott Carter, Margulis found that when they were digitally altered and rearranged to be repetitive, listeners considered the music "not only as more enjoyable and more interesting [than Carter's original nonrepetitive composition], but also more likely to have been composed by a human artist rather than randomly generated by a computer." Margulis concludes, "When we know what's coming next in a tune, we lean forward when listening, imagining the next bit before it actually comes. This kind of listening ahead builds a sense of participation with the music." According to Margulis's research, when there's repetition in music, we simply enjoy it more!

This is true for everything humans perceive; it is the reason we still listen to these iconic compositions hundreds of years later. Repetition is what makes music stand out and endure.

Looking for examples in more recent music history, we can also turn to nearly every song Michael Jackson ever wrote. Beethoven's and Jackson's most memorable compositions can be defined by two very profound and distinct characteristics: bold, repetitive, and stunningly beautiful, emotional *melodies and/or rhythms* soaring over *more complicated*, intricate, and sophisticated arrangements.

Jackson's masterful use of Blocks is why *Thriller* is the best-selling album of all time. Billy Joel's greatest hits album is the fourth-best-selling record.

Michael Jackson used nursery rhyme–type rhythms and melodies in all his songs, from "Don't Stop 'Til You Get Enough" to "Will You Be There." Again, it is the reason his music got attention. Despite his complexity as a writer and performer, it's his melodies (his Blocks) that we remember. No matter what you think of Jackson's character or personal life, there is no denying the global magnetism of his melodies. Well-crafted Blocks grab us by the collar and hook in to us. Blocks don't care whether we want to pay attention. They *make* us pay attention.

Successful songs (think hits by Elvis, the Beatles, Madonna) use multiple Blocks with repetitive riffs, multiple melodies, and countermelodies to help make the music worm inside our ears. These songs stand the test of time. There are scores of genius artists in the world who do not get the attention they deserve because they do not understand the importance of overrepetitive, overdominant melodies.

It is nearly impossible to succeed without giving your audience a Block—the elementary access point that they are all starving for. In music a simple nursery rhyme–type melody, rhythm, or lyric (the sonic equivalent of a central visual image) is dominant and instantly comprehensible to our minds.

It is not a coincidence that three of the most commonly known nursery rhymes, "Twinkle, Twinkle, Little Star," "Baa, Baa Black Sheep" and the "*ABC's*" song, all share the exact same melody. This is the perfect example of how a Block can help us to retain information; it is the sonic equivalent of John Locke's observation of the toy ABC block. Mozart himself is credited with helping to bring this timeless folk melody to a larger audience, using the melody in his Twelve Variations on "Ah! Vous dirai-je, Maman" K.265/300e. It is not surprising that Mozart took an interest in the simple French folk song, as he wrote "Eine kleine Nachtmusik" ("A Little Night Music"), which is also dominated by a repetitive Block melody and is strikingly similar in its unforgettable simplicity.

Sometimes, repetition in music is a deliberate cinematic technique—not just to help us remember or hook us, but also to tell a story. A leitmotif—a recurring musical phrase associated with a person, place, or idea—is a musical technique that was often used by opera composers. Today, it's often used in music for films. The original *Superman* movie with Christopher Reeve, *Jaws*, *Star Wars*, and *Raiders of the Lost Ark* have the most memorable movie scores of all time. It is not a coincidence they were all written by the same Iconist.

The core repetitive nursery rhyme–type melodies are so intrinsically tied to these films that the second we hear them they give us a feeling and take us right back to the emotion and power of watching the film. John Williams did this so consistently it is likely he is a self-aware Iconist, using Blocks with great deliberation and precision. As with Mozart and Beethoven, John Williams's film scores will surely stand the test of time, and people will likely be listening to them in a hundred years as they continue to stir powerful emotion.

Any song may contain up to three dominant repetitive Blocks—whether a melody, countermelody, or rhythm—for it to cut into our senses. Any musician can employ Blocks using this pattern. However, like so many painters, designers, and other artists, few of them do . . . and many sit and wonder why they are not successful or attracting an audience.

Having a unique sound can also be a potent weapon. Take it from Courtney Taylor-Taylor, the lead singer of perennial alt-rock band the Dandy Warhols, who have been together for over twenty-five years and were a favorite band of the late David Bowie. Taylor-Taylor, who writes emotional repetitive melodies, put this bluntly in terms of how he approached his latest album, *Why You So Crazy*:

> For me, emotional singularity or emotional power is more important than all of the other things. Anything that really sounds like another band or record, unless you're doing it well, I find it detracts from your emotional power. You have to be pretty fucking amazing to use pastiche to strengthen your hand, otherwise it dulls your sword. You might like it but it blunts your emotional power of being transportive and emotionally transcending (to) someone who hears it at that moment.

Take, for another example, my close friend Hector Delgado, who is a staggeringly talented hip-hop producer. Hector is a genius, and when he is on two turntables, his hands are so fast you can't see them move. It is like watching the speed and dexterity of a classically trained pianist. Over his long career, Hector has produced tracks for Jay Z, 50 Cent and G-Unit, Eminem, D12, Kendrick Lamar, TDE, and what seemed like an endless array of hip-hop and pop superstars and labels—yet no one knew his name. Not unlike the fighter Chael Sonnen's early struggles in the world of MMA, Hector lingered as maybe the most successful yet (proportionally to his prolific work) unknown hip-hop producer in the world for nearly two decades.

I have always looked up to Hector and have often gone to him over the years to get advice and help on not only my art projects but on life. One day he came to me frustrated and expressed that he wasn't getting the up-front money and recognition of some of his contemporaries and asked me why I thought that was. Quite honestly, I was uncomfortable giving my opinion considering how much I admired him, and I told him I would rather not. He insisted. I reluctantly explained to him that he was acting as a kind of cowboy for hire and that he didn't have his own unique sound—his signature Block'd style. I explained to him that guys like Timbaland and Pharrell Williams were hired and paid for *their* sound and that he, Hector, was being hired to give the artist what *they* wanted. I told Hector that if he settled on a signature repetitive sound, his Block, people would find him. He told me he already had stuff like that.

Hector started focusing on more ethereal, cinematic, emotive soundscapes with beats laid out over heartbreaking '80s pop hits with his postmodern sensibility. His sound crystalized, and today Hector is one of the world's most famous producers. Working alongside superproducer Danger Mouse, he coproduced one of the most successful albums of 2015, A$AP Rocky's *AT.LONG.LAST.A$AP*, which debuted at number one on the Billboard 200. Hector's beat-driven, smoky balladic rhythms worked seamlessly with megastar A$AP Rocky's ethereal sound of cloud rap. When I asked Hector how he eventually found his style, he simply said, "I think we all gravitate toward the things we are exposed to. I am a child of the eighties." Hector has received, and continues to receive, an avalanche of press and acclaim and is now a superproducer in his own right.

The artists that do succeed on a popular or mass-demand level **always** use Blocks—**highly repetitive dominant melodies.**

Let's use another example from popular music. The multi-platinum rock band Rage Against the Machine is widely known for one signature song, the first single on its 1992 self-titled debut album. Despite three more records over a decade that saw the band flourish creatively and raise its profile with fans, the song "Killing in the Name" remains Rage Against the Machine's standard and is considered one of the most influential contemporary youth anthems against racism and police brutality.

The song doesn't contain a traditional structure. Instead, it relies on a series of impassioned and repetitive melodic statements. In fact, every lyric is repeated over and over again, with the phrase "killing in the name of" aggressively proclaimed at least five times, as the hook and one of several Blocks in the song. The song initially focuses on the chant "And now you do what they told ya," with lead singer Zack de la Rocha shouting the lyric almost twenty-five times throughout the course of the five-minute song. This deliberate repetition transforms the phrase "now you do what they told ya" into a another Block and invests it with emotion. The impassioned lyrics command attention. The song gives the listener one Block statement to connect to at a time; it doesn't give any other choice.

Whether or not we personally feel disenfranchised, none of us want to be told that we are puppets just doing what we're told (that is why it resonates emotionally with so many). And after building to a climax, the song culminates with a defiant twist on the iconic lyric, a Block, as de la Rocha rhythmically repeats, "Fuck you, I won't do what you tell me!"

Rage Against the Machine was one of the most influential hard rock groups of the '90s, and its success was neither dumb luck nor coincidence. Tom Morello, the band's lead guitarist, and cofounder alongside de la Rocha, is a Harvard graduate with a degree in social science. Despite the aggression and ardent simplicity of "Killing in the Name," I imagine de la Rocha and Morello worked very intentionally as they crafted the single.

"I was actually shocked," music producer Garth Richardson told *Spin* magazine in an article examining the song's impact twenty years later. When the band first shared the track with him, Richardson recalled, "I thought it was an anthem. From way back then until now, every kid still feels the actual same way. Every kid hates their parents when they're 16, 17 years old." The lyrics connected to the universal desire of teenagers to assert their independence and avoid being controlled.

Indeed, the repetitive simplicity of "Killing in the Name" allows for instant connection, but once that connection is made, potential fans are then willing to listen for the intricacies and the message beneath the surface energy and explicit lyrics.

We've been able to have our cake and eat it too. Every song, every T-shirt, is absolutely a pure expression of what we want to do. And it connects.
—Tom Morello

Global phenomenon Radiohead has sold over thirty million albums around the world with little to no radio play. On nearly every song, across nine full-length albums, singer Thom Yorke commonly repeats a simple, nursery rhyme–type dominant melody—a Block—over and through the entirety of every song, from the beginning of the album to the end. It is the bold, exhaustive use of Blocks in repetition that has propelled Radiohead to be one of the most successful, immediately recognizable bands in the world, even though listeners can't always understand some of the lyrics he sings. The aggressively repeated melody, like Rage Against the Machine's repetitive phrases, captures the listener and doesn't let go. Blocks give the audience no choice but to stop, take notice, and imprint. Blocks are powerful. We can often remember decades later melodies we've only heard a few times, and as with all other Blocks, they can bring mass information and memories along with them.

Just like Yorke, Michael Jackson used repetitive, brazen, aggressive Blocks to pull us into every one of his songs. They are why "mama-say–mama-sa–mama-coosa" sung loud over ten times is so addictive and why Madonna's "Like a Virgin" and Beethoven's *dun–dun–da–dun!* have stood the test of time. How many incredible breakthroughs have we missed out on, or are we missing out on, because unsung geniuses and innovators didn't know to use Blocks?

Now, to be clear—not everything is meant to be screamingly simple. Arthur Russell and John Cage are artists I love. Many of you may have never heard of them, and they are certainly obscure compared to pop superstars like Britney Spears. Russell and Cage weren't striving for mass appeal as their be-all, end-all; they were experimental artists. These guys knew who they were. Everyone should know what gets attention and make a choice.

If an artist doesn't understand the power that a Block melody carries, they might be less heard and not know why. The legendary Quincy Jones has a single-minded, sacred view of the absolute authority of melody. "Melody is king, and don't you ever forget it. Lyrics appear to be out front, but they're not; they're just an accompanying factor."

In understanding Blocks, the choice to be heard is there for everyone, no matter what they do, rather than leaving it up to chance. Blocks are tools and should be seen as such, like a painter might choose a color or a composer might choose a chord progression.

> ### *Melody is God's voice. It's clothed by lyrics, but melody is God's voice—that's the power.*
> ### *—Quincy Jones*

The lesson here is that if you lead with too much complexity—whether it's in a fruit jam or a musical jam—you'll lose that microsecond in which someone will subconsciously decide to stay engaged with you or reject you and move on. Presenting a bold Block up front allows you to offer a wider and wider array of choices *after* your audience has already connected to what you are trying to say.

This is true for music, business, art, and even the relationships we will build with people throughout our lives. *Uniqueness* and *emotion*, whether visual, musical, or conceptual, serve to accelerate the attention they get and the speed at which something becomes iconic.

THE DREAMER AND THE FIGHTER

14

Constant repetition carries conviction.
—**Robert Collier,** *Riches Within Your Reach*

"I have a dream that one day this nation will rise up and live out the true meaning of its creed: 'We hold these truths to be self-evident . . ." In his lionhearted speech from Washington, DC, in late August 1963, Martin Luther King Jr. urged the United States to live up to its potential as a truly free and equal society.

These are enduring words indeed, but let's examine *why* Dr. King's famous words reverberate to the core even after decades, becoming imprinted upon us as one of the most potent collections of words in not only American but world history. What makes them instantaneously recognizable, after more than fifty years, is the two Block phrases that Dr. King uses in the latter half of his speech. "I have a dream" and "let freedom ring" are both used seven to ten times in repetitive, nearly identical ways, in what is a fairly brief speech. Dr. King uses these Block phrases approximately every eighty-five words.

Dr. King's Block declarations—"I have a dream" and "let freedom ring"—help you recall the other important, specific sections of the speech. These Block statements follow the exact same natural laws that enable us to instantly recognize Beethoven's most famous compositions or the Seven Wonders of the World, and it's the same process by which we can conjure up vivid mental pictures of Van Gogh's works. Singular, monolithic, overarching, dominant concepts, in repetition, just work, whether they are words or melodies, messages or paintings. This is just how we mechanically and automatically perceive things from the outside, take them in, and store them in our mental vaults. As one reads or listens to the speech, the Block statements provide repetitive anchors within the much longer text:

I Have a Dream

I have a dream
I have a dream
I have a dream
I have a dream . . . I have a dream
I have a dream . . . I have a dream
I have a dream

let freedom ring
let freedom ring . . . Let freedom ring . . . Let freedom
ring . . . Let freedom ring . . . Let freedom ring . . . Let
freedom ring . . . Let freedom ring . . . Let freedom ring.

"And when this happens, when we allow **freedom to ring**,
when we let it ring from every village and every hamlet, from
every state and every city, we will be able to speed up that

day when all of God's children, black men and white men, Jews and Gentiles, Protestants and Catholics, will be able to join hands and sing in the words of the old Negro spiritual:

Free at last! Free at last!
Thank God Almighty, we are free at last!

The bare words "I have a dream" or "let freedom ring" are enough to bring upon anyone a rush of complex ideas and emotions about civil rights, justice, and equality. Dr. King's two iconic phrases help a vast amount of intricate and historical information to imprint on and permeate our brains. The Block phrases have become Icons that can bring to mind not only the singular cadences of the preacher's speech but also the entire history of the civil rights movement.

Your short statement Block phrase, like a pack mule, will carry a world of complexity, if it is instantly perceivable and repeated with emotional intent.

Whereas King used Blocks as an anthem for peace, on the other side of the Atlantic, just over two decades earlier, an English statesman aroused an entire nation to rise up in the midst of wartime desperation. On June 4, 1940, British prime minister Winston Churchill spoke to the House of Commons in an effort to rally support for the war against the Nazis. Wittingly or not, he used Blocks and delivered what many believe was the most powerful speech of his career. The famous closing lines went like this:

We shall go on to the end. **We shall fight** in France, **we shall fight** on the seas and oceans, **we shall fight** with growing confidence and growing strength in the air, **we shall defend** our island, whatever the cost may be. **We shall fight** on the beaches, **we shall fight** on the landing grounds, **we shall fight** in the fields and in the streets, **we shall fight** in the hills; **we shall never surrender.**

The phrase "we shall fight" is the Block, and its repetition reinforced Churchill's unwavering stance, firmly lodging itself in the minds of listeners. The idea of defending yourself is universal, linking all the way back to the primal "fight for what is right" urge in all of us.

Whether it's the fight against tyranny in Europe or the fight against a bully down the street, people respond positively to the idea of standing up for what's right and opposing a clear wrong. By keying his message to this universal theme, Churchill was able to invoke emotion in anyone in his audience. Although this brief passage is a small portion of a much longer speech, his use of repetition is what makes the entire speech memorable and is how we refer to the speech today: "We Shall Fight on the Beaches." The speech is 3,774 words. He only says "we shall fight" seven times. It's his closer. That brief repetition of a well-crafted, emotional Icon is all it took to assign a name to one of the most powerful speeches of the twentieth century and carry its sentiment.

Even if your duties don't carry the gravitas of wartime politics, or if you happen to be a pacifist, there's a lesson to be learned from Churchill. Research published by the Association for Psychological Science and in the *Journal of Experimental Social Psychology* has shown that when a point is repeated in a presentation 70 percent of participants positively revise their initial position pertaining to the repeated point of view.

Think about the life's work and words of Susan B. Anthony, Mahatma Gandhi, Aung San Suu Kyi, or any of the thousands of iconic activists whose endeavors were equally as convicting and powerful, but whose speeches haven't been remembered? Nelson Mandela is a prime example of these world changers whose messages have *not* been immortalized in the way King's or Churchill's have. The eminent and legendary Mandela gave scores if not hundreds of impassioned public speeches, and freed a nation, but he didn't use Blocks, and we are all the lesser for it. **As uncomfortable as it can be, get comfortable with repetition. Your audience will remember you all the better for it.**

It really is this simple: ideals, concepts, or art Block'd or Icon'd are the most effective tools to get others to stop, pay attention, remember, and appreciate complex details. Facts, memories, and emotions often contain a staggering amount of information compared to the simple Icon that calls them forth. As we know from elementary toy blocks, the human mind naturally wants to connect the complex to big, bold, simple ideas and objects—things that are as eye catching and as clear as a road sign.

Like hearing a familiar melody from your childhood, a repetitive Block within a speech or presentation can instantly deliver vast amounts of emotion and details from earlier parts of your life, or carry these sentiments into the future. The same is true of other sensory experiences, in which memories are driven by the sense of smell or taste. This is how Icons work. Icons are the carrier device for the complex, beautiful, and important experiences in the world.

PART THREE

ROAD SIGNS

The best books . . . are those that tell
you what you know already.
—George Orwell, *1984*

When it is a matter of life or death—like a school-crossing sign or a poison label—we instinctively use Blocks to communicate. Distress calls, emergency response signals, street signs, and safety labels are just a few ways we speak to one another using Blocks. We use them in an attempt to get attention, quickly relay complex information, and let others know that there is something more substantial going on behind the veil.

We rely on these signs as Block-based Icons because they instantly communicate that a barrage of motorized steel may be rushing toward us, or that if we consume a dangerous chemical we'll become sick or even die. Obviously, without recognizable symbols, critical information could not be conveyed fast enough.

As a society we're very comfortable using these principles when we design street signs or warning labels on everything from heavy equipment to cold medicine. It's obvious that they work, yet we don't realize how their power can completely transform our day-to-day lives and personal and professional aspirations.

Imagine crafting a sentence or a meaningful idea so that it had the same impact as a warning label. The effort would pay off immediately by improving the visibility of your artwork, music, or any other idea you wanted to stand out. Because your Block or road sign may be the only hope of communicating in a world with too much in it, we need to craft it with purpose.

Ironically, we actually use almost every trick of language from George Orwell's dystopian nightmare *1984* every day for the public good. When he portrayed his dark, futuristic society (now in our past) using simplistic communication to exert control, what Orwell didn't relay is that *all* information is commonly transferred this way, not just manipulative propaganda. As Orwell declared, anything that is repeated enough—if it is monolithic—even if preposterous, will eventually force its way into the mind. Block'd information is not inherently nefarious; it's just the way human beings perceive and retain information coming at them. It just is. Our mind gloms on to Blocks regardless of the nature of the content.

Road signs don't just protect us from danger. They also help us get to where we want to go. Imagine you're on an urban stretch of interstate. Like in São Paulo before the ban, there are so many billboards and exit signs jumbled together, you can't distinguish what's important. On a highway like this we would only notice the big, broad, bold, green road signs that explicitly tell us where we need to go. We would only follow the sign that points to the location we are trying to get to, or the place that speaks to our needs. The sign that is bigger, brighter, clearer, and more authentic than the other signs is the only one that we will see and that will give us confidence. If it speaks to our desires, we will follow the sign that's a beacon of clarity in a sea of confusion.

Blocks also enhance your credibility because statements that are clear and obvious can be easily tested for veracity. When you understand the best way to construct your Block no matter your medium, you will effectively relay even the most complicated of ideas faster and with far greater force. A compelling Block stands out like a stop sign in the bottleneck of technology-driven communication, and because it stands out, and represents something that we need, it captures and magnetizes the attention of its intended audience.

Using a road sign to communicate what you do and how and why you do it is the most effective way to communicate in our current landscape. If you don't use a road sign, the person you are trying to reach is likely going to get off on another exit—even if you are their desired destination.

Another important lesson to take from road signs: Blocks can work no matter how many other Blocks exist or how common they are. The Block, the road sign–like structure, has simply tapped into what human beings spontaneously gravitate toward. Road signs and warning labels work regardless of how many billions there are in the world because Blocks tap into our primal, instinctual way of taking in the world.

Internally, we don't just prefer—we *crave* detailed communication to be connected to these simple, monolithic shapes and concepts that we can instantly and easily understand. If the locations inside exit signs on a highway weren't consistently presented on massive green rectangles, we would overlook them and miss our exit. This may seem simple, but it is startling how many of us lead with muddled messages or try to reinvent the wheel when we are trying to grab attention, or get what we want, from those that we feel can benefit from us.

The future of all engagement is an information superhighway that we are all hurtling down. We want to turn off at the right exit. Having more information thrown at us than we can possibly process means we lock on to the signs we think will help us get where we want to go. People only get off on their own exit and will reject information that doesn't relate to *their* journey. This is important to remember: when we're driving somewhere, we're not going to change our destination just because another road sign looks nicer. And if you're trying to reach an audience, you're unlikely to reach one that wasn't already looking for what you have to offer.

So marquee, marquee, marquee EVERYTHING. Blocks need to be marqueed massively or they will not work. THIS IS HUGE. People are looking for a road sign. Give them one. State outright the problem you solve or result you achieve. Like the plumber who states outright, "We repair what your husband fixed."

You will need to distill your promise down to its essence—its Block—and you will need to be willing to repeat it ad nauseam. Most important, you have to do it in a way that corresponds to the direction that your drivers are already headed—their primary emotional concern.

The future of messaging depends on us being able to find each other in an overcomplicated, information-polluted world. Your sign might be a jumble, or a concise monolithic Block, or something in between. You may have what you think is a road sign right now, but does it speak directly to your desired audience's primary concerns? Or is it so busy there might as well be nothing on it? Are you just throwing out random words in a desert?

Even if crudely (but steadily) applied, the principles of Blocks and their primordial laws of human perception will help elevate any one of us above the throng.

It's essential to speak to your intended audience in bold, consistent ways that correspond to the signs they are looking for. To ensure you are being heard, your sign must be oversized—huge like a stop sign, really huge—with a repetitive and clear message, containing only facts that your target driver can digest in an instant. You must say it HUGE at every customer touchpoint. People will only respond to the art, music, design, and ideas they are already looking for. Your road sign just helps them to see it.

MAGNETIZE

16

A good teacher, like a good entertainer first must hold
his audience's attention, then he can teach his lesson.
—**John Henrik Clarke, "A Search for Identity"**

Stopping to "smell the roses" might seem like a mundane act, but the cliché
carries a meaning that is very powerful for human beings. Stopping to smell the roses has long since become a metaphor for
taking the time to fully absorb something and enjoy it.

As it happens, that is exactly the goal of a true Iconist. You
are attempting to get someone to stop, look at you, and engage in
a focused relationship with what you have to offer. Interestingly,
like any cliché that's been around a long time, stopping to smell
the roses has developed an instant conceptual meaning, through
repetition, that is vastly more complicated than what it sounds
like on the surface.

By now you know that the abundance of choice in the world
makes it extremely difficult for your audience to see you. If they
do manage to connect with you amid all their other options, do
they really see you clearly?

We all need to start thinking like Iconists.

The dilution problem can be partially solved by decreasing what you decide to present first to the world. By limiting your options to what you offer up front, and using intelligent, emotional, aggressive, authentic Blocks as entry points to stand out, you can hook your audience. Making this up-front connection pulls them into making a commitment to discover the more complex aspects of what you have to offer. Which means that, even if you have a complex idea or a robust product line, you should still use Blocks. It is just about determining what you want to lead with.

To start using Blocks, you need to start looking at the world from the point of view of the person you are trying to reach.

What are you, your business, your brand, your art, or your cause known for? How are you remembered, if at all?

Begin with what you do, say it transparently, say it repetitively, say it emotionally, and say it as big or as loud as you can. Otherwise, it will be as if you never said it at all.

You want to limit any major up-front communication to one to three Block statements or visual images altogether.

If you lead with one to three targeted visual or emotional Blocks and present them with more complicated data later, you will find that your audience is able to absorb more of the specific or technical information required to make a decision.

The following made-up ad is a crude but clear example. On the first page is a bold central image relating to your product, service, or idea. Hovering above or below the image is your Block statement, which speaks to the emotional needs of your audience. A bold, transparent Block statement shows your audience that you understand them and are willing to say it, and say it

ARTISAN AUTHENTIC EUROPEAN

Our artisan jam is made with whole fruit based on the exact same methods used in Europe for hundreds of years. With no added sugars and just a hint of tartness, we strive to give you a flavorful, delicious experience with our authentic, rich, sweet and robust jam.

loudly. This boldness communicates that you are committed to what you are about.

Limiting yourself to a few Block choices creates an access point and magnetizes attention. Random and busy communication absolutely begets rejection and leads to obscurity. The things your audience cares about ring true to them. Putting what they care about up front builds instant credibility that will render your audience more willing to look at your complex information.

The jam in the image on page 155 is emotional to those who love it, especially if you understand and speak directly to why they love it. (This example takes up just one page, but if you have multiple pages, make sure you repeat your Blocks, boldly and profoundly, at the top of each page and keep your choices to a minimum.)

If you were to present the same brochure with a list of all your different jams right up front, you would've lost those customers. They would have been overwhelmed and repulsed. You gain customers and interest in your message only by what you present at the first glance.

It's important to keep in mind that a Block or Icon *is not a slogan*. It's a statement of purpose or a result you achieve. It tells your customer that you are committed to *their needs, interests, or desires*. This fosters immediate credibility because it tells your audience you took the time to understand *them*. If your Block contains the content that your potential customer or onlooker is emotionally concerned with, and it is said large and loud enough, it takes on a whole new meaning.

If you've truly figured out why jam lovers love jam, it's essential that you craft your Block in line with that concept. And if you nail it—getting your Block just right—it will resonate emotionally with jam lovers. The problem is, most people who craft these messages don't really understand *why* their customers love jam. Instead, the jam purveyors are more concerned with *what they did* to create the jam. Which is about themselves, not those they are servicing.

"It's the number one mistake designers make," said heralded footwear designer D'Wayne Edwards in an interview: "They don't think about the consumer, they think about themselves first."

D'Wayne grew up in Inglewood, California, in the heart of South-Central Los Angeles during the 1970s. He lost two of his brothers before their time—one from illness and the other in an accident. Despite those hardships, he had a good mom who encouraged all his pursuits, including his love of sports. As a young boy, however, D'Wayne soon found that he wanted to draw his heroes, professional athletes, much more than he wanted to emulate them on the court or field.

D'Wayne is unique in everything he does because he is suspicious of anything conventional and ignores anything in life that is not effective. This mirrors the philosophy of martial artist and philosopher Bruce Lee in the way Lee saw martial arts and life itself. It is no surprise that D'Wayne admires the legendary fighter and innovator. As an innovator, philosopher, and artist, Bruce Lee had the ability to look deeply into accepted convention and change it for the better.

> ### *Adapt what is useful, reject what is useless, and add what is specifically your own.*
> ### *—Bruce Lee*

In his childhood, D'Wayne loved to draw powerful, poetically graceful athletes. For some reason, he started gravitating toward the shoes that his favorite players were wearing. He found that the footwear was the most complex part of his drawings. By the time he was twelve years old, D'Wayne stopped drawing athletes altogether and was only drawing their shoes.

Though the sneakers of the late '70s and early '80s were flamboyant and iconic, the profession of the hip athletic shoe designer didn't exist yet. And the nature of shoes as streetwear or a form of self-expression for America's youth culture had not yet been realized in the collective consciousness—that is, as fashion blog MR PORTER reported, until Run-DMC's smash hit with the 1986 sneakerhead anthem "My Adidas."

There's a fabled story in which Russell Simmons, the cofounder of Def Jam Recordings and manager of Run-DMC, invited Adidas executives to a Run-DMC concert at New York's Madison Square Garden at the peak of the group's fame, in the mid '80s. The story has appeared in the *Village Voice*. When the dynamic group launched into the hook of "My Adidas," ten thousand kids started waving their shoes in the air. This immediately resulted in the Adidas execs writing Def Jam a check for $1.5 million for the band to officially endorse their shoes. One could also say that the event was a Block *moment* for Russell, and he used it to get the attention he deserved as an arbiter of hip-hop and pop culture.

The success of this song marked a timely shift toward sneakers as a true form of street fashion, and the age of the sneakerhead (sneaker collector) was born. The opportunity to design shoes for the world's elite athletes, musicians, artists, and global youth culture began to take hold, becoming a sought-after creative professional pursuit.

Meanwhile, after being turned down for a job at the Foot Locker at Fox Hills Mall in West Los Angeles a total of six times, seventeen-year-old D'Wayne finally got a job through a temp agency as a file clerk at the international headquarters of shoe-maker LA Gear. After he'd toiled for a year in accounts payable, he noticed a suggestion box where any employee could leave notes about how the company could be improved.

Every day over the next six months, D'Wayne put a sketch of a shoe in that suggestion box—lateral, no angle, straight-on side view—*suggesting* that LA Gear hire him as a full-time shoe designer. Eventually his sketches made their way to LA Gear's CEO, Robert Greenberg. Now, this was the late 1980s, before personal cell phones were commonplace. Still, it must have been shocking to hear a teenage file clerk summoned over the company-wide PA system to meet with the CEO of what at the time was one of the most famous shoe brands in the world. D'Wayne knew his bold designs were going to upper manage-ment, but he couldn't have predicted that very public announce-ment asking him to report to the founder's office. D'Wayne was hired, and at nineteen became the youngest professional shoe designer in the world.

By the age of twenty-three, when most kids are just getting out of college and trying to figure out what to do with their lives, he was made head shoe designer at LA Gear. He went on to spend eleven years at Nike (where he was one of only eight people ever to work on and design the Air Jordan) before eventually walking away from the corporate world.

Today D'Wayne Edwards is hailed as one of the greatest ath-letic shoe designers of all time. He is based in Portland, Oregon, America's shoe design and manufacturing mecca. He started the revolutionary footwear design academy Pensole, now the most respected, innovative, and successful shoe design academy in the world. Regarded as the global authority on shoe design education, he teaches design classes at MIT and lectures at Harvard, and after just four years with Pensole in operation, *Fast Company* named him one of the hundred most innovative people in business.

In essence, D'Wayne noticed that shoe companies were having a hard time finding consistently trained and talented designers. In what is now a $50-billion-a-year industry, D'Wayne saw there was a problem but also a massive opportunity. In founding his academy he created opportunities for talented younger people all over the world who didn't otherwise know how to break into shoe design. "I could see what was wrong in the field. The issues in the industry and the issues of design education, and the disconnection between the two. The students were stuck in the middle," D'Wayne says.

D'Wayne knew the practical reasons why the creative end of this juggernaut of an industry was breaking down. Having followed a previously untraversed career path, he knew how to improve this flawed and broken system of creating and finding qualified designers. Innovation like this rarely comes from inside the establishment. Instead, it comes from unique thinkers like D'Wayne who have not been assimilated by the machine, who are willing to take risks and stand tall in what they know to be true, even when faced by an economically powerful (but flawed) apparatus.

D'Wayne has always been an Iconist. His command of Blocks and how to stand out is at the foundation of his success, his academy, and everything he does. He passes this knowledge on to his students. D'Wayne encourages in all his students the same design-a-day cadence that got him seen, as well as insisting on the straight-on, lateral, no angle, side-view approach—like you would see at a Foot Locker—as a prerequisite for all work submitted by applicants, who come from all over the world. According to D'Wayne, "Seeing design straight on allows you to focus without distraction. It allows you to see the essence and unique qualities of the individual artist you're looking at. Anything more pushes you away." What D'Wayne is describing here is a Block, the anatomy of what makes something iconic.

Undistracted, instantly perceivable communication can contribute to powerful messages. D'Wayne's number one objective is to prepare his students not just for work in the footwear industry but also to *communicate* in the real world. "[When] these kids talk about their designs in 140 characters with abbreviated words, that doesn't work in the real world," he says. "Getting them to understand that their verbal communication is just as important as their visual communication is critical. And even the visual communication needs to show that you're a clear thinker and that you can communicate with or without words. I try to get them to imagine that their portfolio is a comic strip because a comic strip has very few words in it. If you can create a visual presentation that uses very few words, or if the words you do use are massive in size so you get right to the point, then you're a better visual communicator than everyone else. Also, things that are oversized in expression tend to have more emotional impact." Spoken like a true Iconist.

Iconists like D'Wayne Edwards who use the power of Blocks to galvanize their audiences have been present throughout history. But we are just now defining them and bringing their iconic work to light in order to learn from their example. Mozart, Frida Kahlo, Martin Luther King Jr., Andy Warhol, Michael Jackson, and other giants in their fields all used these techniques, whether they knew it or not. None of them were perfect, but they eventually mastered the skill of standing out in a crowded field. They are geniuses not because of the complexity of their works but because of their understanding and desire to use simple, repetitive communication boldly, over and over again, to bring their audiences into the full complexity of who they are. There are so many of us that would be elevated if we were willing to do the same thing. Repetitive simplicity is a major part of genius and is what makes almost anything great.

Just go ahead and communicate to your audience with one to three Block statements. Give them a road sign. Committing to that road sign tends to feel a bit uncomfortable because we know others are going to see it, and we don't want to get it wrong. Fear of failure or rejection is the enemy of greatness and connection. If we let it rule, we won't create our Blocks with enough boldness for those we want to attract. We will hide, without even realizing it, in the busyness of our offering to avoid potential rejection. The tragic irony is that, before we even taste rejection, we are often denying any potential for success, connection, and engagement by not Iconing our offering. Most of us would rather be safe and busy and fail to engage rather than be loud and possibly get it wrong.

We shouldn't play it safe. By putting your Block statement or imagery up front, you always and immediately grab your audience . . . like one married couple did in a small midwestern town almost a century ago.

In December 1931 the young pharmacist Ted Hustead and his wife, Dorothy, wanted to move to a small town where the young family could afford their very own store and go to daily Catholic mass. The company's website tells the story of how the couple came to the town of Wall, South Dakota, which had only 326 residents and a Catholic church for them to attend. It was just what they thought they wanted, so Ted purchased Wall Drug with his relatively modest inheritance of $3,000. Not long after, however, Ted realized just how small, remote, and "busted broke" his new hometown was—theirs was a little business in a little prairie town. One afternoon in the backroom apartment they had built in their store, as they listened to the weathered jalopies pass by on US Route 16A just behind the shop, Dorothy decided to share an idea to get more customers to come to the store. "Well, now what is it that those travelers really want after driving across that hot prairie? They're thirsty. They want water. Ice cold water! Now we've got plenty of ice and water. Why don't we put up signs on the highway telling people to come here for free ice water? Listen, I even made up a few lines for the sign: Get a soda . . . Get a root beer . . . turn next corner . . . Just as near . . . To Highway 16 & 14 . . . Free Ice Water . . . Wall Drug."

Dorothy Hustead was literally saying out loud the simple finite intersection of what Wall Drug could offer and what their desired audience might want or need the *most*. In the company's history on its website, Ted reflects, "The next weekend our son and I went out to the highway and put up our signs for free ice water. I must admit that I felt somewhat silly doing it, but by the time I got back to the store, people had already begun showing up for their ice water. Dorothy was running all around to keep up. I pitched in alongside her."

Dorothy had come up with a literal road sign that spoke directly to the foremost emotional and physical concerns of the people she was trying to reach—travelers who needed a rest and refreshment. Their business took off, even during the peak of the Great Depression in a lonely and remote town. Its signs could be seen around Europe during World War II as a reminder of home and beacon of hospitality for the troops. Today, Wall Drug has become a multimillion-dollar legacy, yet all of its signs are still hand-painted, ice water is always free, and servicemen and -women are greeted with complimentary donuts and coffee in appreciation. And their billboards still advertise Wall as the "Ice Water Store"—Dorothy's "free ice water" Block remains the store's Icon. Before "going viral" referred to anything other than a physician's diagnosis, Wall Drug's brand virality went global. Wall Drug's signs spread across the state, and the store's loyal shoppers took signs all over the world, from GIs taking them to the streets of Europe during World War II to customers holding up the signs at the Great Wall of China and the Taj Mahal.

Road signs and warning labels bypass all the business and communication overload of the modern world. They give us something to see and connect to. We make one by finding that

ONE thing—despite the actual complexity or breadth of our work—that intersects with what our customer *actually* cares about. In the case of the Husteads, their successful road sign was not any of the goods they actually sold to make a living. This is the power of crafting the correct Block. Blocks create virality. Today, Wall Drug still attracts around two million visitors a year.

Transparent, emotional road signs need to replace any and all self-promotional claims. I'll put it another way:

Saying how great you are = **BAD**
Focusing on the concerns of others and where that
intersects with what you actually do = **GOOD**

That's where the use of Blocks, especially in repetition, comes in. When we start looking to distill our work down to one to three up-front Blocks, we begin to understand the fundamental changes we need to make *to ourselves and our own work* if we want others to truly see us in this overcrowded world.

SIGNALS

17

Come out with your unique signal and don't always be compelled to go the common way. That is called innovation.
—**Israelmore Ayivor,** *Shaping the Dream!*

There are two black guys who grew up in humble circumstances, in different parts of the country, who have become known for Block *concepts* with which they are each iconically associated. These concepts have become more recognizable than their names. These singular *concepts* precede them, serving as each man's *signal*, and have propelled both of them to unlikely success. Success that honestly should not have been possible.

These two men do not know each other, but both, unwittingly, Icon'd themselves, leading with who they were through their work and art with a singular passion. Their unique and individual stories show how having a *singular concept* that represents who you are *up front* and unapologetically can help make you accessible to a vast audience.

Kevin Carroll was abandoned by his parents at six years old as a result of poverty and addiction. Today in his fifties, Kevin has lived a remarkable life, and a singular concept has come to define his astonishing career: a red rubber ball, the kind of red rubber ball we all played with on elementary school playgrounds.

A few things about Kevin: He speaks five languages, including Czech, Croatian, Serbian, and German. He went from being a high school athletic trainer to a college athletic trainer to the head trainer for the Philadelphia 76ers in just five years. His words have appeared on over seventeen million Starbucks coffee cups. He has spoken before the United Nations on the importance of play in developing countries and what we in more developed countries can learn from it. Eventually, after participating in the Olympics as a physical trainer for the Yugoslavian Olympic team, Kevin was recruited by Nike, where he was asked to invent his own job title to be a connector and amplifier of the Nike brand. He worked as the "Katalyst" (the K is for Kevin) at Nike for over ten years, then finally left to become one of the most successful international public speakers and a respected agent for social change.

According to Kevin, play is as universal a language as music and is fundamental to human connection, adaptability, productivity, and creativity. Kevin travels over two hundred days a year evangelizing play as a catalyst for social change, speaking to schools, corporations, and nonprofits all around the world. When Kevin is in a developing country, he will trade a brand-new soccer ball to the local children he meets on the street in exchange for one of theirs. (Kevin has had his own line of soccer balls with Molten—one of the world's largest ball manufacturers—imprinted with his own special symbols conveying play, energy, and curiosity.)

In his travels across every continent, he has found people of all ages playing with soccer balls so threadbare that the leather

INDONESIA

MEXICO

UGANDA

MOZAMBIQUE

USA

AFRICA

has been worn away to the thread. He has collected soccer balls made from banana peels, yarn, coconuts, and even compacted garbage. Kevin's artifactual sports balls are on permanent display at the Aspen Institute.

Kevin says his collection of soccer balls from around the world represents the universal human desire to play, regardless of whether we live in prosperity or want. People will always find a way to engage in play.

Kevin knows a lot about the science of play and believes in his heart there is no other thing on earth quite like the ball. In a casual conversation, he will go into great detail about Friedrich Fröbel, the German innovator and teacher who created the concept of Kindergarten. Fröbel laid out a series of sequenced gifts that children should receive to support their early development. (All these gifts, as Kevin explained to me one day, are versions of toy blocks.) The first gift is a soft *ball*. According to research, the word "ball" is often among a baby's first. We are chasing balls from the moment we can crawl and some of us continue chasing them until we die. That primal power of the ball signals how important play really is to humans.

Kevin loves all sports and debated what balls he should focus on to communicate his message of play in his first book. Soccer (his favorite sport) is big everywhere except in his home country of the United States. Football, baseball, and basketball are really only mainstream in America. So Kevin settled on the red rubber balls that are ubiquitous on every primary and elementary school playground across the world. The book Kevin wrote at Nike was a tribute to the power of the ball and play, and told his story of overcoming abandonment and poverty to reach what should have been impossible heights. Called *Rules of the Red Rubber Ball*, the book used the red rubber ball that we all chased around in elementary school as a metaphor for *chasing our purpose in life and speeding up and amplifying human potential.*

The book's original design was elaborate, inside and out, constructed with thick cardboard and textured red rubber in the shape of a ball on the top. He hired a renowned design firm, Willoughby Design, to communicate the playful sensory spirit of his message. He found a rogue printer in Vancouver, BC, Met Fine Printers, who were willing to go all in on his unusual rubber-and-cardboard book.

Kevin was already one of the most sought-after public speakers globally by the time he left his brand amplifier position at Nike. Today, he is represented by the leading international talent agencies for public speaking, including Washington Speakers Bureau and the Creative Artists Agency—who represent former presidents and movie stars. There seems to be an insatiable demand for him and his message at every kind of company or institution. Having been in such high demand as a speaker while at Nike, Kevin began to realize his sole mission and purpose in life: he needed to leave Nike to evangelize the power of play around the world.

Kevin believes deeply that when we chase our purpose in life it changes us, and makes us better, more effective people. When we play as children, we do it unselfconsciously. Kevin believes that by using play as a tool for social change we can get back to chasing what fulfills us as adults. So it follows that if we all chase our purpose—our red rubber balls from childhood—as individuals, our society will improve collectively.

Kevin decided to pursue a major publishing deal to amplify his message. Yet despite having successfully sold his self-published *Rules of the Red Rubber Ball* at his talks, he couldn't get any mainstream agent or publisher to take it. Again and again, he heard,

"It is too expensive to produce with its thick cardboard and red rubber," or "The message is laid out in a way we've never seen before." Most had never seen a book that looked like a children's book with grown-up content. His favorite statement of rejection was "It is overdesigned and too creative."

So Kevin just continued his travels, selling his self-produced books at his speaking events. He was completely perplexed that no big publisher would buy it when he saw it resonating with such an incredible cross-section of people at his events. Eventually, he was approached by sports goliath ESPN's new book-publishing arm; they took on the project, and the book continues to sell more than a decade later. It is passed around by tens of thousands of people as a kind of living artifact containing knowledge on how to overcome obstacles. It is the kind of book you feel compelled to pass on after you read and experience it.

Kevin is recognized wherever he goes as the "red rubber ball guy"—a Block that has completely overshadowed his career at Nike, his military career in which he learned three Slavic languages, his Olympic experience, and his being only the third black head athletic trainer ever hired in the NBA. And yes, the book's message about play is powerful. However, if the book did not so obviously lead with the pure simplicity of the red rubber ball, it would not be what it is today, nor would it be the universal symbol of Kevin Carroll, his signal, and his legacy to the world. When people recognize him on the street or in an airport, they yell, "You're the red rubber ball guy!"

No matter our work, if we can be represented by some overarching, immediately perceivable concept or symbol—our Block—it will propel us farther and faster than we would ever get if we lead with a complicated or unclear message. It will serve as your signal, getting you seen and remembered, providing just enough to get people to look deeper. As we see with successful Icons, when we repeat our Block, we can get it to carry with it the full complexity of who we are.

Let's look at another signal. A singular concept has come to define Donwan Harrell's astonishing career—denim work jeans that resonate with people of every creed, color, and class.

Donwan Harrell is an artist who grew up working-class in Virginia. His father worked as a naval ship repairman and his mother was a seamstress. He has risen to become the most successful independent denim designer on earth. Donwan's aggressively distinct signature washes (the way any designed denim is weathered, aged, and stained) have become the powerful signal for his brands.

Donwan is more of a denim archaeologist than a traditional designer. He created his designs by regularly traveling to remote parts of the United States on three- or four-week road trips, collecting and cataloging the different ways people wore their denim workwear. He would observe how paint might splatter or mist on jeans from a paint booth at an auto body repair shop. He noted down how someone loading feed at a farmhouse or working in an underground mine might create a distress, or a unique wear pattern, on the worker's "uniform." Or it could be how oil and grease stain and dye a pair of jeans worn by a mechanic or a farm worker. He became fascinated by how denim, with manual labor and scars, wears in ways that are as varied and unique as a fingerprint.

After a trip, he would head back into the studio to design his forcefully stained and distressed denim. Donwan uses complex techniques to create patterns of stress and wear that go into every unique denim wash. For Donwan as a designer-creator, these washes must always be based on, or inspired by, real life. No matter how rich or poor or accomplished we are, there is an impulse in all of us—regardless of age, gender, or where we live in the world—to wear clothing that tells a story; we still value work done with our hands, despite the virtual nature of our current times. We also, as a collective, tend to love things that show our journey or, at the very least, an imprint of a hard day's work done well. For this reason, Donwan's washes are often *emotional* to look at.

Donwan's hard work and attention to detail paid off, for him and for his suppliers. Donwan was the first American to go to Japan to manufacture selvedge denim on their old shuttle looms. (For years, many fans of his product actually thought that, Donwan was Japanese.) Selvedge is produced around the world, but Japanese denim is often considered superior because the expensive, durable, flowy material is produced in limited quantities on vintage looms, resulting in a character unlike any other textile. Despite the fact that hardcore denim enthusiasts—"denim heads"—had sworn by selvedge for decades, it hadn't been sold in larger, mainstream stores. Until Donwan's washes came along, Americans were not willing to shell out $300 to $500 a pair for jeans. Producers and importers of selvedge the world over have benefited from his innovation.

Second, and most important for us, Donwan has become known for and synonymous with his special washes. It is how he and his work are recognized by the retail buyers of the major department stores and the people who love to wear his special product. The brand he founded, PRPS (short for "purpose"), is a luxurious jean beloved by celebrities and artists, including culture makers like Jay Z, Brad Pitt, and David Beckham. (The battle cry for the brand is "Bruised Never Broken." For decades he named all his jeans after 1960s and '70s muscle cars, which he collects but doesn't always tell his wife about.)

There is true irony in the fact that the jeans he designs to look "worked in" cost hundreds and, in rare cases, over a thousand dollars. A few years ago, Mike Rowe, television host of *Dirty Jobs*, called him out publicly when he saw the price of Donwan's dirt-covered Mud Jeans. "I took umbrage, (that's right—umbrage,) [sic] with the emergence of jeans with fake mud on sale at Nordstrom's for $400," Rowe said.

Donwan's washes are distinct and instantly recognizable to his audience as the most authentically "lived in, worked in"–looking denim one can buy. More than "denim designs," Donwan's signature style, his Block, is his washes. Donwan's decades of dedication and work have created a signature Block that, through repetition and consistency, now associates him with the most intricate and *realistic* denim washes in the world. Just like the criticism of Beethoven, what Rowe is offended by with Donwan's denim as *paintings* is the distinct Block that separates and amplifies Donwan as a unique artist. The Block has been such a successful signal for Donwan that after he left the brand he founded he received big unsolicited investment offers and many inquiries to design for others at established global fashion houses. Donwan decided to embark on a new denim venture, ARTMEETSCHAOS, and the signal helped the leading retail buyers to fully embrace and covet his new brand within months of launch.

In fact, the success of Donwan's Block (the washes) transcended the success of his popular brand. Donwan shows how, if we can become known for one thing that makes us special or resonates with those we wish to engage with, our Block message, science, style, or idea can be a gateway to sustained success.

ARROW AND SHAFT

18

The saddest aspect of life right now is that science gathers knowledge faster than society gathers wisdom.
—Isaac Asimov, *Isaac Asimov's Book of Science and Nature Quotations*

I know a man named Bluegrass Biggs whose life might be even more interesting than his name. Bluegrass grew up dirt poor in rural Oregon and was raised along the banks of the McKenzie River. He spent much of his early childhood living out of a tent and a van. What Bluegrass Biggs's life has become is something that is completely unpredictable and a testament to the uniqueness, power, and ingenuity of the human spirit—he is the kind of guy that glows.

Today, "Blue" has a PhD in chemical engineering and runs BiggsB, now one of the country's leading bioscience consultancies. He splits his time between Raleigh, North Carolina, and Nara, Japan. He also owns race cars, sponsors a race team, and has three patents pending for his GPS application called Spotter, which may be the most accurate racing technology in the world. Spotter helps improve safety for race car drivers and helps them improve their track performance. His real-time analytics (on a mounted cell phone) allow a driver to see how they are driving and gaining or losing on any given stretch of track and to make adjustments moment to moment when they hit that same stretch of track on their next loop around.

When it came to BiggsB, however, the benefit for potential clients wasn't as obvious as Spotter's benefits for drivers. When I first met Bluegrass, I shared with him the principles of Blocks. He went on to reverse engineer his consultancy and how it presented itself. Most of the leading pharmaceutical and medical device companies that hire BiggsB, no matter the country they are located in, struggle with the morass of regulations that govern their industries and are concerned about whether they are accurately operating by the rule book. One mistake could mean a fortune in fines. But they also do not want to have a consultant come in and disrupt their operations or alter the "vibe" in their workplace.

Because of his upbringing, Bluegrass has a unique sensitivity to understanding how to make something as complicated as regulation a lived-in, easy process. Bluegrass came up with the monolithic Block DEMYSTIFYING REGULATORY COMPLIANCE. The sophisticated bioscience, medical, and pharmaceutical companies that hire Bluegrass are often mystified by the labyrinth of regulatory compliance they are required to observe. That is why Bluegrass's Block is so powerful to them. After leading with the Block, he then offers an abundance of specific content in terms of how easy and nondisruptive it is to hire BiggsB. He only employs consultants that put clients at ease and never make them feel like they are getting audited by the IRS—which is a common predatory tactic of his competitors. He realizes that his customers don't want to pay a company that makes them feel uncomfortable. Bluegrass has mastered the arrow and the shaft—the relationship between the radically simple and the more complex information that Blocks carry.

What does this mean for you? Say you were an interior designer. If your client said, "I want a French country home," you should then use the phrase "French country home" as a Block as you talk to this person in real time. People are *emotional* about where they want to live, and since your potential client communicated a desire to live in a "French country home," you know that this idea is emotional. You would then relate all the details in your client pitch to this emotional statement, exhaustively repeating the Block phrase "French country home" throughout any verbal sales or promotional presentation. The Block is the head of the arrow in your message; the rest of the presentation is the shaft—the complex information that backs up your Block. You had better deliver the best French country interior ever or your success will be short lived. The Block phrase should serve as an internal directive or monitor for what you will deliver. When you get this right, not only do you create a comfort level but you are also confirming and grounding yourself in what you need and what is expected. This is not about being Orwellian but rather about listening and being transparent up front, to your potential client and to yourself. In order to stand out, you need to do what you promise—and do it differently or better than others.

People become professionals and create companies to solve problems. Problems are, by nature, emotional. The key is to understand that no matter what you have to do or say, your job is solving a problem for someone, and that's going to be *emotional*. Listen to those you are trying to convince. They will hand you the Block that will affect them most on a silver platter. Most of us just aren't listening.

Don't shy away from this approach even if it seems reductive or repetitive. Sharing too much information about other specific or technical details will more likely cost you the job, because it will distance your potential client from the emotional reasons behind their actions. If you want to ensure you stand out and connect to your client, constantly repeat and use the term "French country home" as the arrowhead in your messaging, and build all the details about the job to this emotional cue. Your client is also likely to be more relaxed, comfortable, trusting, and much more likely to pay attention to the plans and specs that matter to both of you.

If you used that term in repetition, your client will pay more attention—and will remember your pitch better than your competitors'—because the Block phrase "French country home" is simple, instantly perceivable, and what your client cares about emotionally. Your *knowing* use of this phrase will change the way your client sees the details, allowing them to remember specifics that they might normally forget. The specific details are now connected to the Block, so when the Block is remembered, so are the details.

Regardless of talent, an inexperienced designer who has the ability to repeatedly use Blocks and create Icons in the minds of clients when pitching the details of a job will likely be more successful than an established designer who does not use Blocks. No matter how eclectic or unusual, no matter how complicated or mundane, if you look for it, every piece of communication has a Block that can make the message distinct and make it stand out. Your information will be better perceived and remembered by your target audience when you use carefully crafted short emotional statements in repetition based on what matters to the person you are communicating to.

This means knowing the perceived personal benefit to your listener and using it as your Block. The Block commands a response because, as discussed, professions and companies exist to solve problems.

Up to this point, we've focused on Blocks—the bold and monolithic image, statement, or message that grabs attention in a *blink* (shout-out to Malcolm Gladwell). But it's more accurate to think of your full message or product as an arrow, with both a sharply pointed head and a long shaft.

Imagine trying to be an archer, shooting arrow shafts with no arrowheads. You would never be able to hit your target with consistency. On the other hand, imagine trying to launch an arrowhead without having a shaft to fit in your bow. You might as well be skipping rocks across a lake; your aim wouldn't be true, and the arrow would miss the mark. So if you want your Blocks to work every time and to remain in the minds of others, you must connect the monolithic, simple, bold Block to the intricacy that follows right behind it.

With his Block, like with Wall Drug and their *free ice water*, BiggsB taps directly into the *emotional concern* of its clients: the fear of missing something, getting something wrong, or just being overwhelmed by the compliance laws. Bluegrass follows with copy that explains that he has created the world's most user-friendly, comfortable way to achieve compliance and includes plenty of information about how it works. That one-two punch has created a market where BiggsB is constantly fighting to keep up with overwhelming demand. Using Blocks can and will drive you far past the competition and make you the indispensable choice.

There's another example from the tech world that perfectly shows how a Block statement—one that addresses the primary concern of the audience—created instant demand. Intel had a new chip called vPro that offered a ton of robust features. The trouble was, it originally promoted its new chip with *all* its unique capabilities out front, including fifteen different features. Like so many of us, Intel developers were so proud of *everything* they had accomplished that they wanted to present every bit of it to the world, all at once, with equal volume. They led with the whole forest of their work and no one who needed to care could see the tree that mattered to them. The message about vPro became indistinguishable noise rather than the symphonic harmony they heard as the creators.

Despite Intel's best efforts, the product was failing to take off. And this was in an increasingly competitive marketplace where new manufacturers were offering similar products to its business-to-business market at lower and lower prices. Intel had to find a way to maintain its price integrity while retaining its market share.

When vPro's sales teams were asked what the customers *actually cared about* in the new product, they all agreed that their customers were primarily concerned with just one unique security feature. It was the ability for company laptops in the field to be controlled, monitored, and, if need be, cleared remotely. Naturally, this is a major concern for large corporations with lots of proprietary information. This concept became their Block, the monolithic idea, the singular billboard, that any audience can latch on to and grasp instantly.

Intel pivoted its product message, leading with a Block banner statement and promoting it outright: "Leading-Edge Security for an Unwired Workplace."

It turned out that when companies immediately understood vPro as a security product, they wanted it and needed it. Through Intel's Block product message and brand it narrowed the scope of its offering down to a singular monolith—the one that absolutely mattered most to its desired consumers—and repeated it tirelessly. It did this despite the complexity of everything its new product *could* do. Its sales teams still promote vPro's other features and details, but only *after* they present their Block, up front, bannered across the entirety of their product messaging.

It is the combination of the emotionally relevant message said in an unusually oversized way (the arrowhead) that grabs attention. Remember, customers are on a superhighway looking for your product or service with an endless number of exits. They will get off at the recognizable, bold, oversized exit sign that most corresponds to their needs. Once you understand this, you can race past your competition. And if your competitors do this, too, you better have something more urgently needed than they do to make a road sign out of.

So, whether it is a painting, a photo, a revolutionary idea, a company ethos, or a chip, our success in an overmessaged world starts with the arrowhead, a road sign, the Block. Add repetition of the Block, and we have a foolproof system that all of us can get right every time. Intel repeats this message about vPro anywhere and everywhere it can, at every customer touchpoint—it is why it has been so quickly "Icon'd" into the minds of its customers.

Think of your giant Block arrow as having a disproportionate head that is much, much larger than the shaft—at least the way it is presented up front, visually. Once the arrow strikes and slices through its target, then the shaft becomes just as relevant as the arrowhead (the Block). The shaft causes the arrowhead to fly, cut deep, and stick in the mind.

Leading with simplicity eliminates distraction and cuts through the human resistance to data overload. Complex information attached to a Block causes that information to become readily available in the mind.

BLOCK

Once your BLOCK is repeated enough times to your audience it will enter the mind and become an Icon to them. A Block is just an Icon waiting to happen. It is something you repeat that will quickly create an Icon in the minds of those you are trying to reach.

What's essential here is to constantly repeat your Block, alternating that first one to three Blocks with more complex or technical information. In the end, the interspersing of the complex information and the Blocks causes your message to bypass distraction, stick, and then remain in the mind.

In order for Blocks to work, all brochures, advertising, websites, *everything you aim at your audience* **must have massive marquee lettering and imagery** so that it can be mentally processed in a glance. This is the access point, the entryway, the road sign and portal to all that you want to communicate. Not using Blocks is like walling up the doors to who you are and what you actually want to say.

Even if you have created the perfect Block to captivate your audience, if you do not say it large enough for them to see, it won't matter, and it will not cut through.

Advertisers—the professional message makers among us—have been trying to solve the puzzle of consumer fickleness for

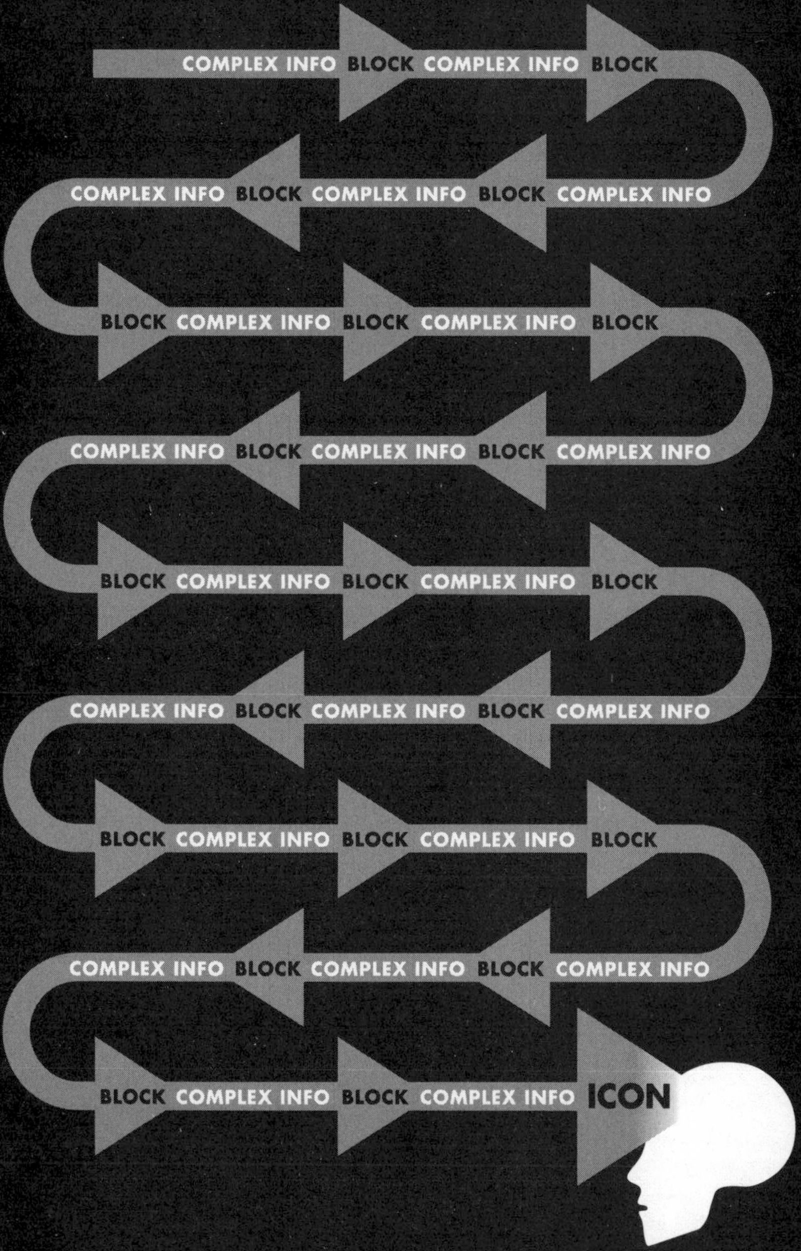
COMPLEX INFO BLOCK COMPLEX INFO BLOCK
COMPLEX INFO BLOCK COMPLEX INFO BLOCK COMPLEX INFO
BLOCK COMPLEX INFO BLOCK COMPLEX INFO BLOCK
COMPLEX INFO BLOCK COMPLEX INFO BLOCK COMPLEX INFO
BLOCK COMPLEX INFO BLOCK COMPLEX INFO BLOCK
COMPLEX INFO BLOCK COMPLEX INFO BLOCK COMPLEX INFO
BLOCK COMPLEX INFO BLOCK COMPLEX INFO BLOCK
COMPLEX INFO BLOCK COMPLEX INFO BLOCK COMPLEX INFO
BLOCK COMPLEX INFO BLOCK COMPLEX INFO ICON

centuries without really understanding the mechanics involved. This is why we see so many ineffective slogans that don't really mean anything to us. Ad firms know they need to boil a message down to something that can be perceived instantly, yet they rarely know how to distill it into something we truly care about. They understand the importance of the arrowhead, but underestimate the power of the shaft. Or they craft a message that's too focused on complex details, leaving out the driving force of the arrow in favor of the weak impact of the shaft. Or they just create a senseless, inauthentic arrowhead for lack of something better. Be authentic, transparent, and direct through Blocks, and you will have a hard time not crafting an effective Icon.

Earlier I said that a Block or Icon is not a slogan. That's true—but a slogan can sometimes be a Block.

A slogan is a group of words that may or may not get others to care about you, your work, or your company. A Block is an emotional arrowhead that goes straight to the heart of what your potential audience truly cares about. If your slogan does this, then you can call it a Block.

One of the best slogans ever (which also happens to be a Block) was the original FedEx statement from 1978 to 1983: "When it absolutely, positively has to be there overnight."

It was a unique approach because FedEx spelled out exactly the problem it solved for customers, in the most literal way. At the time, it was unusual for a company to describe the end result of its service. The ad campaign was also emotional; before the days of email and the internet, FedEx and only a couple of other services were the only way to send sensitive or original information quickly, and the phrase "absolutely, positively" underscored

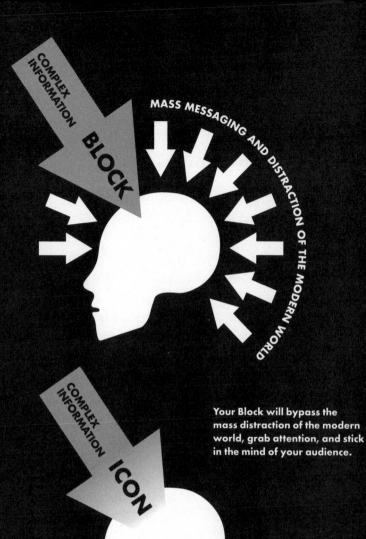

COMPLEX INFORMATION

BLOCK

MASS MESSAGING AND DISTRACTION OF THE MODERN WORLD

COMPLEX INFORMATION

ICON

Your Block will bypass the mass distraction of the modern world, grab attention, and stick in the mind of your audience.

the urgency customers *felt* when sending a package overnight. FedEx's message is a statement of fact, not a tag line.

Today there are plenty of companies that offer similar delivery services, but FedEx has been so effective in Iconing itself that many people still simply tell you to "FedEx" your package when it needs to get somewhere overnight. Markets change and times change, so it also is possible that your Icon may need to change with time. Sending something overnight now has a somewhat diminished importance in our digital world. The key is just to say what you do for your desired audience outright and everywhere, with brazen repetition.

When we see an ad, text message, or email, it's there for a second and then quickly fades away, like drops of water evaporating in the midday sun. Emotionally resonant Blocks will help your message stick.

Ask yourself: What do you do for your customers? What problem do you solve for them? What result does your product or service achieve? What need does your art fill and what type of person is it going to attract?

Look at your promotional materials: How big and boldly are you stating your audience's emotional concerns? Is your message loud or prominent, like a banner taking up an entire page? Whatever the medium of your messaging, are you communicating BOLDLY with your central imagery—like Warhol or Van Gogh or the "Red Rubber Ball" guy?

BREEED

19

The Snowball Effect

Indescribable . . . Indestructible! Nothing Can Stop It!
—**Tag line for 1958 screenplay** *The Blob*

A well-composed, easily repeated Icon is kind of like the manifestation of the "Blob" from the eponymous pulp horror movie of the late 1950s. Each time the Blob consumes something, it grows bigger and more powerful. With Blocks, repetition makes your Icon grow bigger, more dominant, and more influential.

Blocks **R**epeated **E**xhaustively **E**verywhere **E**quals **D**emand = **BREEED**

BREEED, or the Snowball Effect, is my formula that allows us to employ Blocks and use them right away. You can literally BREEED an Icon using Blocks. Any person in any field can BREEED anything they are creating, sharing, or doing right now to generate attention and demand.

Deliberately repeat your Block everywhere, all the time, and your Block will become an Icon. If you create a Block to represent you, your product, service, idea, message, or art, and you repeat it everywhere, it will BREEED instant interest and engagement.

Any Block aggressively repeated will imprint upon the mind of any intended audience. It will BREEED an Icon.

Like a snowball rolling down a mountain, the more your Block is repeated, the bigger, faster, and more powerful it gets. This is equally true for a ten-minute speech as it is for a ten-year promotional or sales generation campaign.

Remember, repetition is counterintuitive—it works even if it feels weird and uncomfortable to be unduly repetitive. Yet, it's always best to repeat the exact same (or a very similar) phrase or image. There will be times when it may sound weird or strange to repeat yourself. Do it anyway. If you want to be subtle because you feel that exact repetition would be too contrived, find different ways of saying the same thing to Block your concept—think of it as your signal.

Roadtec is a small company in Chattanooga, Tennessee, that invented a very big machine. Just a few years ago, the company was only selling one or two units per year and was barely scraping by, despite the genius of its innovation. Its machine is a rock crusher and gravel road forger, all in one. You can roll this machine over a rocky, impassable old logging road, and it will expertly turn it into a smooth, drivable road as it goes by grinding the rocks in its path into crunchy, dusty gravel. It can be used by timber and mining companies to make almost any sketchy pass crossable.

In just a few short years, however, Roadtec has grown from a small family-run company and managed to expand its product line and exponentially increase demand for its crushers and pavers. Its growth is in large part due to the work of PowerPR, a rare PR firm that has used repetitive Block headlines for decades. This is the Block they used for Roadtec:

Gravel Road Repair: Don't Bury the Problem, Crush It

This phrase may mean nothing to you, but to a person that is responsible for drivable roads in the forest service or in a logging company it is *highly emotional*. PowerPR takes one base article and repeats it everywhere across a range of publications that focus on a single demographic.

A PowerPR article consists of a single Block statement followed by an information-rich article, and they then run that single article in repetitively targeted magazines for three to six months at a time. The header for the articles they create—the Block—always matches the client's offering to the primary emotional concerns of the client's intended customer. They will put one article in a specific category of industry-related magazines—at the same time, with the same header. The intended audience is then more likely to see the same article and header multiple times across multiple locations. This repetition carries power, and helped to BREEED Roadtec into a prosperous enterprise, where previously it had been invisible.

Even though a Block is remarkably enhanced by the receiver's emotional connection to the Block, there are plenty of symbols without an emotional punch that over time have become Icon'd strictly on the basis of repetition. Eventually, any statement repeated enough, as Orwell proposed, emotional or not, will create a connection. In the Western world, names like Kleenex, Band-Aid, Xerox, and Coke have all been repeated so often that they have become synonymous with the products themselves.

Language experts have a term for this: "proprietary eponyms," meaning words that once were proprietary brand names or trademarks that are now used generically (like FedEx in the last chapter). But how do you become eponymous? Repetition. There is a shortcut, though. The reason for using BREEED is to speed up the process and control the outcome in moments—creating an instantly perceivable, emotionally resonant Icon with deliberation.

A Block can gain traction with an audience in a nanosecond for the same reasons that it will still be recognized over two, five, or even ten thousand years later. Smaller individual Block representations *snowball* into a larger singular representation, becoming iconic.

It is common to think that something has to be old or famous—a symphony by Beethoven, or a mysterious monument like Stonehenge—to work its way into our collective consciousness. But the age of something and its level of fame have little to do with why we remember it.

The way you communicate your concept determines how others view you and your ideas. It determines whether you have credibility and whether you are chosen above others competing for the same attention.

True Iconists shape and sharpen their Blocks so that they not only cut through the clutter of mass distraction and personal dilution but lodge in the minds of their audience as quickly as possible. Deliberate repetition of a bold, simple Block does wonders to speed up what for a long time was considered a random, uncontrollable process.

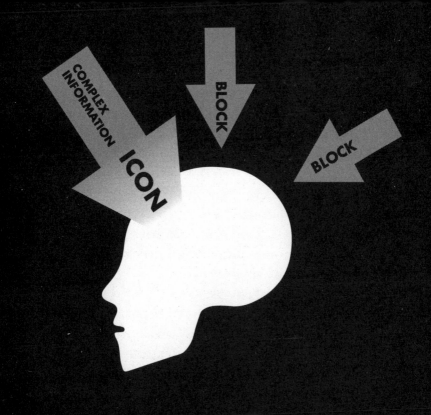

YOUR ICON REINFORCED THROUGH REPETITION

Even the simplest images can become laden with complex information with repetition over time—think of the Golden Arches. Before you can even recall Mickey D's name, you can probably list its most popular treats and practically smell and taste the last thing you ordered there. You can recall the jingle or visualize one of its commercials. The iconic symbol of the massive Golden Arches delivers. When you're driving down the highway and you see that Icon, you don't need to be told anything else. The entire menu is already flashing through your mind. The Icon represents much more than just the name; it's the entire menu of the McDonald's experience. The fact is, one simple thing can pack a wallop of information. This truth is transformatively powerful if you choose to employ it.

When you see a picture of a loved one, you associate that person's face with a sea of events and emotions that you experienced together. Those memories and feelings come rushing in, in an instant, whether we want them to or not.

An Iconist will speak in simple Blocks, but also, when possible, in an unexpected way. Uniqueness is like candy for the mind. An unusual Block that represents your unique self will intrigue the recipient, demanding even more instant attention and comprehension. In circumstances where it might be inappropriate to repeat the same thing over and over, Block the sentiment—the emotional subtext—of your message instead, and repeat that sentiment as your Block.

BREEED doesn't just help your audience to find your product or idea. It also helps *you*. The act of funneling specific communication into a continuously repeating, finite point is very stabilizing and enhances your own personal composure significantly. You will feel more positive in your own self-promotion and communication, whether it is written, spoken, musical, or visual. Being consistent and repetitive makes us feel more certain of the ground we are standing on because it is also our own communication to ourselves about what we have chosen to do and say, and powerfully reminds us *why* we have chosen to do it. This is the purpose and integrity in a company or person, and the anatomy of a personal style in an artist. So when we repeat it, we can *feel* that it will cut through, and we like the way it feels.

PART FOUR

PERFECTION IS DECEPTION

20

There is no religion higher than Truth and Righteousness.
—**Mahatma Gandhi,** *Ethical Religion*

What if I told you that I have never made a mistake? What if I proclaimed to you that I am the best dancer who ever lived and have always been the best and won everything I have ever attempted? I am an Olympic-level figure skater and a tenth-degree black belt in a martial art that I invented called Mustard Kun Do.

Your first impulse would be skepticism, and you would quickly conclude that I am a liar—and not only a liar, but also maybe a little bit crazy. Self-obsessed advertising comes across as crazy. Yet it's all too common to see companies peddling their wares through ads that carry on about how great they are. The result? In the digital age, companies that prop themselves up as "perfect" lose their intended audiences' trust.

As far back as 1999—long before the siege of social media and before internet advertising was going full steam—the former chief marketing officer of Coca-Cola, Sergio Zyman, recognized this problem. "TRADITIONAL MARKETING IS NOT DYING—IT'S

DEAD!" Zyman proclaimed in the conclusion of his bestselling book *The End of Marketing as We Know It.*

He went on to say,

> Mass advertising has lost its ability to move the masses. Technology has given people many more options than they had in the past and created a consumer democracy. Everybody has a thousand choices for any product they might want to buy, and there are a million different products competing for their wallets. So marketers increasingly need to find ways to speak to customers individually, or in smaller and smaller groups. With so many choices, each customer has many factors that weigh in his or her decisions, so marketers have to find the reasons that speak to particular customers' concerns.

How many times have you heard a restaurant claim to have the "best pizza" in town? There are examples like this in advertising for every product and service available. Society has been leery of self-serving advertising claims since the mass proliferation of ads beginning in the late 1960s and early '70s, as Al and Laura Ries noted in *The Fall of Advertising and the Rise of PR.* From beverages to breakfast cereal to cigarettes and financial institutions, the history of modern advertising is full of unverifiable, outrageous self-promotional claims and slogans, like Coke saying their sugary drink "adds life," or Camel's claim that "more doctors smoke Camels than any other cigarette." The list goes on . . . You can find countless examples presented by some of the world's best-known products and brands—a sad reflection of much of the advertising industry's lack of respect for consumers:

"Fresh, wholesome Hostess"—Hostess Cupcakes

"The best a man can get"—Gillette

"Her singing coach advised a light smoke"—Lucky Strike

"A bowl a day keeps the bullies away"—Apple Jacks

"As your dentist, I would recommend Viceroys"—
Viceroy Cigarettes

"No family left behind"—World Financial Group

"Where vision gets built"—Lehman Brothers

Time has revealed all these slogans to be patently false, but businesses and the advertising industry still make assertions like this every day. This comes across as absolutely insulting and repulsive in a world of instant access to information on smartphones. Consumers can check your claim on their phones in real time . . . and they do. Companies need to offer things in a way that is based on the present world we live in. To go on, just glance at the packaging in the candy display at your grocery store. How many sugary treats like licorice, jelly beans, and gummies can you spot with the words "low fat" or "fat free!" on their labels? They may not be fatty, but that doesn't mean these candies are good for you, which is what they are in effect trying to imply.

Several years ago, the *Harvard Business Review* reported on the effectiveness of modern "marketing" programs and strategies by looking at all the leading data on marketing performance.

The findings reveal why many business owners feel the way they do:

- 84 percent of marketing programs actually resulted in less market share.
- Most efforts to get more customers lost money.
- Sales promotions generally lost money.
- Return on investment from advertising was below 4 percent.
- When companies with established products doubled their advertising budgets, they only increased their sales by 1 to 2 percent.
- 90 percent of new products brought to market failed.

Despite the fact that advertising has lost much of its effectiveness, self-loving, narcissistic advertising still affects the way we interact and our ability to believe each other as people—not just when we're trying to land a sale. This is likely a direct result of being bombarded with nonsensical marketing claims. In our minds, claims of perfection *really* have come to be synonymous with lying—a consequence of mass media and relentless advertising that unceasingly pushes unbelievable messages at us and often isn't held accountable for the authenticity or accuracy of its claims. Advertising caused us to distrust anything that sounds self-serving, even if it's true. This skepticism has spread to other areas of our lives. When we talk to our colleagues, our partners, our children, our friends, our bosses, or even our employees, self-endorsing expressions tend to undermine our credibility. We are less likely to believe an anecdote a coworker might tell us at work. If a loved one is telling us a story with any bragging, we are now, after a lifetime of advertising onslaught, more likely to feel repulsed than impressed.

Self-promotion breeds distrust. *Adweek* shared a Gallup poll that showed 82 percent of American consumers distrust big-business claims. And while this has been going on for decades, the ubiquity of the internet has brought it to an all-time high. Regarding the overabundance of ad exposure, the *Adweek* article states, "When you're exposed to that much advertising, it's easy to filter all those aggressive, sales-y messages to a singular, blurry kind of white noise." The same article speaks to the eroded trust in advertising we all feel: "For millions of Americans, advertisers and corporations have become like strangers with ulterior motives—meaning that they aren't to be trusted and aren't worth paying attention to."

We now think perfection *is* deception.

So what does this mean for an Iconist? A person telling the truth only has one story. So whatever you claim to the world, make sure it represents true aspects of who you are.

Authenticity is so important today that tech executive and author Tom Hayes made it the first tenet in his 2014 book *Relevance: Matter More.* If you build your message on an inauthentic premise, Hayes says, it's bound to fail. There's a certain amount of self-awareness and self-discovery that goes into this process.

Hayes writes,

> Too many companies—and individuals—are befuddled by delusion when it comes to identifying their authentic strengths and projecting those strengths through their

brand. It's as if they live in Opposite Land. If their service is wretched, they tell people that they are great at service. If they are selling a mediocre car, they expound on its hip sportiness. Claiming that you are what you are not will obscure the strengths you do have while destroying your credibility. It's a lose-lose proposition. In order to hunt down and accurately tag authenticity, we must first pop the balloon of self-delusion.

There's a great movie from the early 1990s starring Dudley Moore called *Crazy People*. The plot follows a top Madison Avenue advertising executive who loses his mind when his wife leaves him. After spending years creating campaigns that lie to people about the products he sells, he can't live with himself anymore. Moore's character travels to a mental health clinic in a rustic part of upstate New York to recover and gather back his sanity. Because he's the top man at his firm, his boss encourages him to work while he recuperates, but while at the clinic he has an epiphany and realizes that all he needs to do is tell the truth in his campaigns. Other patients in the mental asylum are inspired to help Dudley's character with his work, and they start to manufacture ridiculously truthful campaigns. They come up with pitches like these, which would never fly at a real ad agency:

"If you're risking cancer, shouldn't your cigarette deliver real flavor? Shouldn't something that might make you die really taste great? Amalfi Super Thins. Pulmonary Cancer? Perhaps . . . Flavor? *For Sure!*"

"Buy Volvos. They're boxy but they're good. This is not a smart time to be sexy anyway, with so many new diseases around. Be safe instead of sexy."

"Forget Paris. The French can be annoying. Come to Greece. We're nicer."

"Metamucil: It helps you go to the toilet. If you don't use it, you'll get cancer and die."

Ridiculous maybe, but in our current culture, these joke campaigns are closer to what would be considered credible to most consumers, next to the mass-advertising campaigns that flood our marketplace. We now live in a time where we need to state our primary, truthful intent. Perhaps not as hilariously as the asylum inmates do in *Crazy People*, but with clarity and authenticity. In one telling exchange in the film, two characters banter:

"Let's level WITH AMERICA!"

"We CAN'T level with America, you crazy bastard. We're in advertising!"

We really do live in a different time. Brand loyalty is not what it used to be. American manufacturing has been sent offshore. People don't always buy the same model car year after year, and people don't have the job security with major corporations that they used to. As a result, advertising isn't effective when it just reinforces brand identity. Technology has created access to so many choices that consumers want to feel *they are getting the best option for their money*, not necessarily the most famous brand. Instant access to information, being able to read endless reviews and user experiences, means that consumers will choose what they want based on what they see, and not on what anyone with clearly self-serving motives tells them they want.

And authenticity isn't just about what you say; it's also about what you do. When you develop your Block statement, make sure it clearly reflects what you actually do, not just what you think your audience wants you to do. If you are doing your job with your potential audience in mind, it should be easy for you to authentically resonate. If you can't win others over by being yourself, then, in our current times, you probably need to change how or what you do so that you can be yourself for real.

For a long time, the prevailing idea in the communications industry was to use testimonials, referrals, or a third-party endorsement as an alternative to self-loving advertising because it would help increase a brand's credibility. The problem with that approach is that many people automatically switch off when faced with these tactics, especially given the overuse of paid celebrity endorsements. When very little communication is getting through, being credible becomes irrelevant. You have to be able to be heard in the first place before your audience will evaluate who you are and whether your message has worth.

This simple idea can bring the lofty world of advertising back to earth and restore it to the realm of credibility. The concise and iconic nature of advertising makes the field naturally suited to Blocks. Advertising is by nature repetitive.

With Blocks, you can position your product, idea, or message and make it credible without referrals—as long as there is transparent, truthful, simple, and easily comprehensible information following the Block, to hold and further engage the attention your Block has garnered. If *perfection is deception*, then being up front and authentic in who you are and what you do is imperative. Today it is more important than ever to be transparent.

NAKED

They say I'm old-fashioned, and live in the past, but
sometimes I think progress progresses too fast!
—**Dr. Seuss,** *The Lorax*

We live in an era of radical transparency. Our communication channels not only are more abundant than in the past but also move at a furious pace. We can't always tell when someone isn't speaking from a place of authenticity, but we can almost always tell when they are. Transparency builds trust.

The graphic on the following page represents how much the world has changed in just fifty years, an instant in the stopwatch of history.

Cable news channels are in a constant race to keep us updated from around the world, starting the moment any event unfolds. This competition creates a juggernaut of information and establishes an *expectation* to be constantly informed. Text messaging, email, video chat, and other technologies allow us to create and deliver on-the-spot communications between ourselves and an ocean of contacts. We can communicate instantly, and we expect an instant response.

GROWTH OF AMERICAN COMMUNICATIONS

	1968	TODAY
SENT TEXT MESSAGES	0	2,000,000,000+
MOBILE PHONES	0	279,000,000
INTERNET USERS	0	245,000,000
TELEPHONE LINES	41,600,000	151,000,000
SATELLITE RADIO STATIONS	0	227
BROADCAST RADIO STATIONS	5,158	14,952
BROADCAST TV STATIONS	603	1,783
NEWSPAPERS	13,212	13,670

Ironically, print newspaper technology hasn't changed all that much, so the number of print papers from fifty years ago to today hasn't really changed. What the table doesn't show is the tens of thousands of online news outlets that exist today.

Sources: Census.gov, SiriusXM.com, AmericanRadioHistory.com, Stanford.edu.

The irony is that technology-driven resources like the internet do not always provide the most accurate information, and most people know it. In fact, a survey by Harris Interactive found that 98 percent of Americans "distrust the information found on the Internet." Among their reasons were four fundamental items related to the data deluge:

- 59 percent say too many ads
- 56 percent say outdated information
- 53 percent say information is self-promotional
- 45 percent say unfamiliar forums

Even though we fact-check on the internet, we are still wary of what we find. More specifically, internet-only news sources are considered highly unreliable, with only 12.5 percent of people believing the information these sites publish. Yet faith in traditional media isn't much better. Since the late '90s, long before smartphones, Gallup has been asking Americans, "In general, how much trust and confidence do you have in the mass media—such as newspapers, TV, and radio—when it comes to reporting the news fully, accurately, and fairly: a great deal, a fair amount, not very much, or none at all?"

Only 13 percent of Americans express high confidence in print media, and just a meager 14 percent have high confidence in TV and cable news.

The public's view of the media has changed dramatically since the days of Walter Cronkite and Edward R. Murrow, and we don't need a study to tell us this is true. As I mentioned in the last chapter, it's generally accepted that we mistrust advertising; that's not a surprise. Few would object to the suggestion that no one trusts advertising. What *is* shocking is how this

AMERICAN TRUST IN MASS MEDIA

1997	TODAY

100%

A GREAT DEAL OR FAIR AMOUNT

50%

NOT VERY MUCH OR NOT AT ALL

0%

Source: Lymari Maralis, "U.S. Distrust in Media Hits
New High," Gallup, September 21, 2012.

experience has affected the way that we process *all* mass media information.

The pressure of so much data upon us and the technological advancement to interact with this mass of information has overwhelmed us to the point that we react to too much information by taking in no information, or far less information, while reducing the relative value of the information we do take in. Those 98 percent of Americans who distrust the internet likely still completely rely on it. We are just so slammed with all this content that the internet is the easiest way to deal with the burden. You could liken it to urgently trying to get across town in a broken-down car with a busted-up engine and a flat tire. Most of us would rather not drive a car like that, but we would use it if we were desperate enough. You could say that the information overload forces us into a new way of thinking and working, using reckless measures to cope with the content overload.

What does this mean for you when you're trying to stand out in any kind of marketplace?

When I say that we live in an era of transparency, what I am saying is that our communication channels are so immense and so fast that it's just not worth the effort to try to deceive anyone anymore. Outrageous claims and half-truths don't work in a society where information is easily and instantly accessible. In a world where we can check any claim in a few seconds, for an Iconist it's ineffective to claim anything that you don't *know* to be absolutely true.

A Block is different from a slogan or catchphrase. It could be a statement of your mission or your intent. Whatever it is, it will not come across like an ad if you mean what you say and can back it up. Businesses need to start leading with authentic transparency if they want to keep their customers and gain more. Artists, artisans, and designers need to speak more transparently about their work. Openness and transparency will get you noticed.

Let's take an example from the corporate world. Several years back, Domino's Pizza had an unprecedented full year of stock price decline, and the chain decided to take an honest look at itself. It realized the areas where it was failing. *Bloomberg Businessweek* reported that consumers, in a harsh reality, thought Domino's "pizza sucked" and the "crust tasted like cardboard." So the company cooked up a new recipe and a money-back guarantee, along with a social media and advertising campaign that specifically addressed the concerns of their customers. They admitted to themselves that their global product was pretty awful. They approached the problem in a bold, iconic way.

WE SUCK.
—Domino's

This is the ultimate in transparency—and it completely turned the company around in the middle of a recession. Domino's stock price rose extraordinarily—sixty-fold—restoring the pizza maker to its former glory or even surpassing it. When they stated the truth in an overt, out-loud way, they generated demand that increased their sales dramatically. In just three months from the campaign's launch, they came within three days of running out of pepperoni, and by the fourth month their same-store sales had risen 14 percent on average. Domino's increased its market share from 9 percent up to 15 percent in just six years. Admittedly, after the worldwide financial catastrophe of 2008, many US pizza chains increased sales (pizza being an inexpensive dinner to feed an entire family). Still, none experienced the boom Domino's did in terms of increasing market share, stock price, and demand.

As the investing website Motley Fool reported, Domino's decided to tell the truth about their pizza and vowed to fix it. Whenever we speak to what everyone is already thinking but does not say, we immediately breed trust. Transparency is power.

If transparency reveals your imperfections, believe it or not, imperfection will enhance your credibility. Being imperfect is being human, and in an age of worldwide, often dehumanizing, corporatization, we long for a renewed sense of humanity. Domino's certainly shows us how we feel if we think someone is giving us straight talk. It's magnetic.

There is nothing more credible than speaking plainly and from your heart. Whether you are trying to communicate with your wife or husband, children, benefactors, supporters, or customers, be direct and be transparent. You should just explain why you want them to do what you want them to do and how it benefits them. The gummy bear people could do this by saying, "When you want something yummy, eat a gummy," rather than insinuating their product is "healthful" because it is fat free. I bet they would probably sell more.

Your message must always be authentic. Others won't always be able to tell when you are lying, but they can always tell when you are telling the truth. Transparency and authenticity breed trust. Authenticity is a form of empathy. By speaking from the heart, you are saying "I respect you enough to take the time to understand you." Today, empathy toward others reads as, and *is*, credibility. The opposite of this is continuing to shove a bunch of self-centered stuff at us that we don't want to see or hear.

Our technology-induced expectation of being able to check any claim or review—anywhere at any time—makes us all now expect transparency. And when we don't get it, we feel insulted. It is the same expectation, created by instant, real-time, ubiquitous access and sharing, that launched the Arab Spring in 2009. Here, the lack of transparency by corrupt regimes was unveiled by instant access to information, in real time, by everyone, anywhere, across almost any geography. Nearly all of the protests in this movement were organized on Facebook and Twitter, just a click away from where you read your Yelp restaurant reviews. What the Arab Spring proved is that when people irrefutably know they are being exploited and manipulated, in real time, they will risk death fighting to free themselves from the yoke of oppressive rule. Smartphones and social sharing embolden us to seek, share, and expect the truth.

The current social expectation actually is this: if you're not completely transparent, you're lying. Yet so many in the multigazillion-dollar advertising industry continue to lie to and cajole us, like the march of the wooden soldiers. The truth is, whether we accept it or not, product sales and social justice both now pivot on extreme transparency.

This is not a pontification on honest representation or morality, it is just a statement of fact about the world we live in—a world of instantly shareable, instantly verifiable information. Technology, rather than morality, forces this move toward honesty. You could call it a form of free-market information competition in which the person with the most straightforward and accurate information wins.

Popular research professor Brené Brown has spent twenty years researching how vulnerability fosters human connection. In other words, one or both people being extremely vulnerable in a relationship ensures a deeper connection. Her TED Talk, "The Power of Vulnerability," has almost 40 million views and is one of the top five most viewed TED Talks of all time. I believe the corporate, organizational, or institutional equivalent of vulnerability is *transparency*—transparency about every aspect of your business, internally within your company to your employees and externally outside your company to your partners, audience, and customers who engage your message, product, service, or offering. Being transparent creates deeper, more sustained connection. Because the world has been turned into a glass house by all the information the internet can instantly provide us, leading with transparency shows that you have respect for your audience . . . Though people may not articulate it to themselves, they know when they're being disrespected and resent it rather than gravitate to you.

For an Iconist, the best way to stand out in the forest is to be truthful, clear, and direct. Your real customers will see you. Those who are not your audience won't waste your time or even be looking for your exit sign because it will not be leading to the place they want to go.

If the customers like what they hear, they will also appreciate that the salesperson was observant enough to understand them, and they will likely give their business to the person who most readily presents them with transparent facts. They will also enjoy the fact that they were not hassled in the process. Thanks to technology, this is where customers land. This Icon age likely marks a revolution in the way in which people buy and sell products.

To the onlooker, if perception is deception, then transparency is truth.

Everything in our world involves some sort of a marketplace, no matter what we do—parents, artists, CEOs, managers, engineers, designers, teachers all need to grab attention to be successful in a world where everything is simultaneously screaming for attention. We all become salespeople when we're trying to convince someone to do something, whether we're trying to get our kids to eat their vegetables or our customers to pay attention to our message.

The best way to cross the "no-credibility threshold" is not to work to convince your audience that your claims are legitimate but rather to give people useful, factual, digestible information and allow them to decide for themselves if the information is valid. Because anyone can google you, if you present anything other than the truth, your audience will reject you when they see it on their phone, and you will lose them because now you have offended them. When we are bombarded with too much information and self-promotional claims, we long for others to speak plainly and tell us the truth so that we can make a sound decision.

Being up front and providing simple content in a nonpromotional way creates instant credibility with any audience.

This is what Blocks, or the arrow and the shaft, are doing. They declare your emotional understanding of your audience in a bold way, then get you to back it up with transparent, digestible facts.

Blocks based on transparency cut through the credibility gap so that people don't feel that they need to double-check your claims. Your audience will be in agreement with you immediately because you are being transparent through marquee Block communication that breaks through and reaches them, like a road sign. Transparency and authenticity secure trust.

The trick is, there is no trick. Blocks get you seen. Just present your offerings with concise, bold, transparent, and AUTHEN-TIC Blocks and follow it up with resonant facts—an arrow and a shaft. This is what cuts through.

THE DILUTION GENERATION

22

What every genuine philosopher—every genuine
man, in fact—craves most is praise, although the
philosophers generally call it "recognition"!
—**William James, letter to Henri Bergson**

Many call them Generation Z or iGen. I call them the Dilution Generation—the
children born between the early 1990s and today, during the
rise of the internet revolution. This is the first generation to
grow up with massive media and digital technology as the norm;
they have no knowledge of "simpler times"—times when we
were limited to three channels and not thirty thousand points
of light ceaselessly streaming at us like a blazing sun that never
sets.

In a 2014 interview, advertising executive Mike Sheehan said,
"My daughter was five when she saw her first television commercial. ('What's that?' she asked)." At the time, Sheehan was
CEO of a major advertising agency, having built his entire career
writing and directing TV commercials, but his own daughter
only engaged with online content. Sheehan states, "Getting an

advertising message to millennials and younger will mean a new world order in media."

This group of digitally raised young people is an inadvertent social experiment in an electronic screen–saturated experience. We don't know the full extent of how that technology will change them, but we already see telling signs. For instance, think about how kids now consume music. Thirty years ago, teenagers were extremely limited in terms of how many albums they could buy. There was no on-demand music; your music consumption depended on how much you could afford, or copy onto tape. The only access to new music, beyond the radio and TV, was CDs, vinyl, and cassette tapes found in record stores or borrowed from your friends.

The few available choices tended to limit how many personal favorites a fan would have. Personal economics determined how many CDs one could buy, and for most, it was maybe a few dozen over time that we tended to listen to with attuned and eager ears from start to finish. But in the 2000s kids had hundreds of bands and thousands of songs on their MP3 players or downloaded onto their computers or phones; today, many of them use streaming services and have access to a nearly limitless library. *This, like every other kind of overload, dilutes the connection to and changes the way we perceive individual songs and individual artists.* We engage with music differently when we listen to an album or mixtape from start to finish, compared to when we stream music from the internet through curated Spotify playlists, often not paying attention as the songs change, jumping from one artist to another.

Because the Dilution Generation consumes so much music, on such a massive scale, they don't experience individual albums or songs like their predecessors. If you only had a handful of vinyl records, you would likely know the lyrics to every song and memorize the album front to back. If you had 7,160 songs on your iPod (the average number in an iTunes library, according to the website 9to5Mac), though, you would not experience or engage with each song with the same intensity as you would if you were limited to a small vinyl or CD collection.

Abundance alters the way you perceive things. Kids today have access to countless forests, which means they never stop to fully explore any individual tree. On some level, in different areas of their lives, they're aware of this superficiality. And it doesn't feel great to know you're not fully connecting to any one thing.

The children of dilution feel smaller than any other generation before. These kids have no period in their lives in which they did not live in mass-messaging overload—*dilution*. I believe this permanent sensory overload has given them a constant itch they can never scratch.

The Dilution Generation is in constant contact with others through an electronic device. They can message a classmate across the street or a friend across the world with just one click. But in the end, this glut of accessibility just dulls their ability to focus on parents, schoolwork, or anything else that's important.

Children of dilution are going to have a harder time asserting their individuality, ideas, entrepreneurship, or ability to contribute to the world. The long-term social effects of this are unknown, but you can imagine the internal impact on their feelings of self-expression, personal recognition, and eventually, self-actualization.

The technological world is like trying to make your way through an anthology with a hundred billion authors. There is just that much data.

Anyone can shoot and edit a video on a smartphone for pennies compared to what it would've cost a few decades ago. You would think this should result in more great videos, films, and filmmakers. And while it has allowed some access to newcomers, it has mostly created a bigger sea of mediocrity. The same can be said about the ubiquity of sound-mixing software that turns anyone with a laptop and a mic into a recording artist; we've got an increase in quantity, not quality.

When something is cheap, it requires less investment on every level. When something is expensive, people tend to spend a lot more time preparing and planning what they are going to do with it. The same could be said for businesses or for your own ambitions. Ease and access don't necessarily mean a better outcome.

A limited experience generates a sense of importance, while abundance and volume generally make most things feel less important. This is partly why diamonds are so valuable; they are, when compared to other minerals of the earth, rare. (The iconic slogan "A diamond is forever" also helped.)

What will be the consequence of content overload? How will dilution affect the Dilution Generation, especially when they have no recollection of simpler times, no reference point for a different way of life? Will this generation just connect with less intensity as a whole? Will these hindrances to personal connection lead to a generation of more depressed and isolated young people?

This may sound drastic, but I strongly believe that Blocks have a power that goes beyond merely communicating ideas. In an increasingly crowded world, the connections they allow can help us to be *seen* and understood. In my view, we can trace a lot of the big problems facing our society back to the desire for connection and recognition—and what happens when we don't get it.

Personal recognition and the ability to express ourselves are two of the primary drivers for humans to feel positive and more fulfilled. In my experience with clients, whether they're painters, architects, or businesspeople, when I show them their work as a Block, they are relieved and empowered, mentally and emotionally. (In many cases clients breathe an audible sigh of relief.) The Block is already there—together, we work to chisel it from the body of their work. This is a testament to the restorative power of Blocks, and what they do for us.

Take self-expression away from people or make it harder for them to communicate, and it can have severe social and mental effects. The weird part is that even though most of us feel something is wrong, in terms of our ability to cut through the dilution cloud, we wouldn't necessarily think of our personal dilution as a serious personal or social problem. It absolutely is. Many of my clients and the younger generation of workers I've spoken to feel this very intensely.

It's making our society more depressed and anxiety-ridden because we feel it is harder to be seen and heard personally and professionally. It's affecting us all en masse.

Renowned American psychologist Abraham Maslow defined the highest level of self-esteem, *self-actualization*, as "to become more and more what one is, to become everything that one is capable of becoming." This is the internal life and drive that Blocks instill when you use them. Maslow goes on to say that the "happiest moments" in life occur when we are hit by a great piece of art or deep human connection, making us feel more integrated in the world and more in control of our lives.

We can signal like minds toward like minds, renew lost dreams, rekindle hope and optimism, and rejuvenate anyone who chooses to use Blocks to engage the world.

Understanding how to use Blocks to express your unique gifts in a way that stands out and grabs the attention of others will be even more important for the Dilution Generation—even the worthiest, most motivated, and talented individuals among them. Despite their obvious power (they are out there in the world and all around you, easy to observe), there are so many reasons it can be hard for people to use Blocks and iconic communication as a way of relaying their ideas:

corporate or institutional inertia;

the discomfort of having all eyes on you;

the uncomfortable feeling that comes from saying something simply and repeatedly;

the refusal, fear, or resistance to being simple and transparent; or

not understanding how to craft or deploy your Block.

And yet, right now, too many millennials and Gen Z kids feel like cogs in a corporate machine. And with more and more information overload, these feelings are metastasizing in the mind. This increased difficulty in getting attention is affecting the new generations, personally and professionally, but by the time they realize what's happening, many may already be riddled with anxiety and depression.

The understanding of these prehistoric Blocks and Icons might be more useful to the Dilution Generation than any other group—it will only become more important to communicate with Blocks. The trends that have gotten us to where we are (data proliferation, an app for everything, increasing digitization and competition) aren't going to go away. Blocks will be paramount in the same way we need road signs to guide us. The current and future generations can learn how to direct traffic toward themselves in a culture where feeling lost in the digital void is the new normal.

That said, radical simplicity is not just about success; it is about sanity. This transparency really is the only way to make a true connection in an overcomplicated world. There are people with something to say all over the world who don't understand why they can't grab attention. Just forming and using Blocks creates mental relief internally, even if you have not yet begun to receive the magnetism they generate externally.

The renewal, hope, and reinvigoration that we experience by leading with our simple toy Blocks can have surprising, profound effects on the feeling of any class and can completely reinspire one's outlook on life. In this way, the use of Blocks—the anatomy of what commands attention and creates mental Icons—can help us to recharge and reconnect as humans worthy of recognition.

Blocks carry the power to change how we see, hear, reach,
and connect with everything and everyone around us.
The laws of Blocks have always been there. Now they are codified for anyone
to use to grab attention for any message, art, science, business, or idea.

THE PRIMAL LAWS OF BLOCKS

Codified in *The Iconist*, a Block in any medium is a succinct statement, phrase, image, or design that can be understood instantly.

In **MUSIC**, the Block is a simple melody or a word or lyrical phrase repeated over and over throughout any musical composition or song.

In a **SPEECH**, the Block is a highly emotional or truthful statement repeated over and over throughout any oration, address, or presentation.

In **VISUAL ART**, the Block is an oversized central image, instantly perceivable and unavoidable to the eye—this can be amplified by a distinct, immediately recognizable style.

In **MESSAGING** or **PROMOTION**, the Block is a GIGANTIC banner phrase that immediately addresses the emotional concerns of the intended audience. The banner is then aggressively repeated throughout the technical or complex information you are trying to communicate at every point of customer contact.

In **DESIGN** or **ARCHITECTURE**, the Block is a bold, oversized, high-contrast, distinct, and instantly recognizable shape.

In **CORPORATE DEMAND GENERATION**, it is the core ideological intent of your company, understood internally and externally, that communicates YOUR PURPOSE, the PROBLEM YOU SOLVE, or the RESULT YOU ACHIEVE in a way that corresponds to the *emotional* concerns of those whose attention or business you want to get.

In **BUSINESS**, you create your Block by distilling down YOUR AUTHENTIC PURPOSE and the EMOTIONAL PROBLEM YOU SOLVE or the RESULT YOU ACHIEVE at the intersection point of the primary concern of your desired audience. State it clearly, obviously, and boldly over and over so that it is seen, heard, and imprinted in the mind. If we want a response, we must first message in this MARQUEED, instantly perceivable way to capture attention. It is this bold, declarative, confident statement of intent that instantly builds credibility if it corresponds to the emotional concerns of your customers.

BLOCKS work by themselves with repetition. When you add EMOTION or COLOR or connect COMPLEXITY to a Block, its power of magnetism is always AMPLIFIED—mesmerizing us and demanding our attention.

BLOCKS' Application for **Professionals:**

1. Evaluate and identify your audience's primary emotional concern corresponding to **your purpose, problem you solve,** or **result you achieve**.

2. BOLDLY, MASSIVELY, SINGULARLY address this concern through a visual image, symbol, logo, or an OVERSIZED MARQUEE BANNER Icon statement, whether it is a presentation, résumé, or an email.

3. Stick to it! Repeat and repeat your bold, simple Block declaration **everywhere**.

The result will be transfixing and calming to the onlooker—automatic, organic, attention-grabbing, gripping, and emotionally charged—and will authentically engage your desired audience, every time. Repetition of the Block works for several reasons. Like Melanie Pullen said, a person needs to see a similar image repeated at least three times to get it. This is especially true in a world where we are constantly distracted and overwhelmed by all the messages coming at us. When repeated everywhere, over and over, your Block will also communicate conviction. Last, it grounds you the user in why and what your primary intent is, and that stabilizing feeling is priceless.

Constant repetition carries conviction.
—Robert Collier

With the primal laws of BLOCKS, anyone can now create a near-instant Icon of the mind in any field.

AFTERWORD

On Thanksgiving Day of 2009 a homeless man was arrested for sleeping in Washington Square Park in New York City, where he lived. The man was scraggly and worn out, with matted hair and a bright red beard. He reeked of alcohol and hadn't showered in weeks. He was what most of us would call a bum. His physical state was that of a man who had spent years of hard living on the streets of downtown New York.

In my college days, my grandparents lived in New York, and the city had been my home base while I attended school in London. The downtown park by NYU was one of my favorite spots. I could have easily stepped right over this man as I walked around to watch the speed chess players and the buskers performing for loose change. This man, his face wizened to the point of anonymity by years on the street, would have been invisible to me.

The homeless man was my estranged brother, Danny. I had known him only off and on while growing up on the streets of Hollywood. And I hadn't spoken to him for nine years, not since we had scattered our dad's ashes off the coast of the California shore.

On that particular Thanksgiving morning, it was a drizzly thirty-six degrees. It was the kind of wet and cold that seeps under your skin and into your bones. The cops who had arrested Danny that day had done so on innumerable occasions. It was the cost of rent for a homeless man living in the park. The police would typically cite him with a ticket he would never pay, send him to lockup for a day, and then release him. These particular cops knew him well, and they and my brother were comfortable in their exchange. But on this day they gave him a choice: the police told him that if he would be willing to go on the *Opie and Anthony* radio show and talk about what it means to be homeless in the city on Thanksgiving, the irreverent radio hosts would pay him *and* he would not have to go to jail.

Unsurprisingly, Danny decided to go for the money. At the beginning of his interview, the duo asked him if he had any "hobbies." Danny replied that he was a musician. The politically incorrect hosts found this statement amusing coming from a homeless man, and quickly asked their assistants to find him a guitar. Within minutes, Daniel "Homeless" Mustard began what he called the "anthem of his youth," a staggeringly beautiful rendition of Radiohead's "Creep." The performance was at once ironic, powerful, and strange. It was surreal to watch. The hosts were speechless, even deferential, and obviously moved. What they thought would be a gag turned into an awkward yet poignant moment of deep reflection.

The producers of the *Opie and Anthony* show gave Danny a couple of hundred dollars; he left, bought a bottle of Svedka vodka, and then went and got drunk in Washington Square Park. My brother didn't think anything of it. All he knew was that he had some money in his pocket and the warmth of hard liquor in his belly.

Over the next few weeks, a confused Daniel noticed people yelling at him and cheering at him enthusiastically from cars as he traveled around NYC. People would cry out, "Go Mustard!" or "Hey! Homeless Mustard!" It was a very strange experience for a man who was used to being invisible. Eventually, he figured out that *Opie and Anthony* had posted his cover of "Creep" and that it had gone viral all over the world with millions of views.

Danny became a kind of instant celebrity and had fans in foreign countries building and dedicating entire websites to him. He had to open two Facebook accounts and quickly garnered over ten thousand friends (yes, homeless people use Facebook). He had become a symbol of inspiration to people and had illuminated a part of humanity that we normally dismiss. Danny and his performance touched something deep in people as they recognized the frustration of feeling that others fail to see us for who we are on the inside. Danny had defied this in the most beautiful and heart-wrenching way.

> *When you are homeless, you're invisible to people, like literally. They will step over you, ignore you when you talk, look right through you. It's really a haunting thing to experience every day.*
> *—Daniel Mustard*

In the following weeks and months, Danny received and executed two independent record deals. The coveted music magazine *Spin* published the remarkable story of his rise, and in another article declared his cover of Radiohead's most famous song as one of the top ten greatest "Creep" covers of all time, alongside versions by Kelly Clarkson, Moby, Amanda Palmer, Damien Rice, Korn, Weezer, and the Pretenders. "Daniel brings real fucking pain to this real fucking painful song. He is, to most, an actual creep," it read. He was even tracked down by the producers of *The Voice* and flown to Los Angeles for an audition.

Today, Danny is not rich or even solvent and lives in a halfway house in Brooklyn. His song has over thirty million views and counting. His celebrity got him off the street and free from drugs and alcohol, and he has been sober for over nine years. His homelessness and sobriety counselors asked him to find a relative he could talk to, because, in their expertise, part of the reason he had fallen to the streets was because he did not have any contact with family. He asked me to be that person for him, that person he could talk to. We talk often, and he is amazing. Getting to know Danny (formerly "Homeless") Mustard, my brother, has been an honor.

This is an incredible story, but you may wonder why I'm telling it here, in a book about Blocks. Well, it's been shown that those who grow up in poverty are more likely to engage in a host of self-destructive, high-risk behaviors. According to the *Journal of Youth and Adolescence*, they are more prone to substance abuse, high-risk sexual activity, criminal behavior, and violence. According to research published in *Brookings Big Ideas for America*, the general result of a poor upbringing can be a potent feeling of hopelessness about your future prospects. This is what researchers call an "underclass personality"; it is characterized by a "dark cynicism" and deep internal conviction that your future circumstances hold little to no promise.

Ultimately, our own ability to feel like we have the potential to be fulfilled has a huge impact on our mental attitude and our overall behavior in life. When human beings feel they don't have a chance, they won't even try, or, worse, they will self-destruct or self-sabotage.

The primary cause of paralysis, anxiety, dissatisfaction, and depression in those living in poverty is the feeling that you don't have a chance to succeed in the future, translating to a *general hopelessness*. These symptoms are remarkably similar to, if not the same as, what social theory professor Barry Schwartz has found in victims of choice overload and feeling *diluted*.

I believe that, to some degree, the ubiquity of constant, ceaseless connectivity and messaging in the digital age has brought a pandemic of *hopelessness* upon all of us. I am not trying to bag on the internet. I am a far greater fan than a critic. What the web has done for freedom of information for all—for me, alone—makes its side effects worthwhile. That being said, I think if we don't engage with the internet consciously, the effects of feeling diluted will make us feel paralyzed by the prospect of even trying, and therefore make us hopeless about the future. When I give public talks, millennials express this to me consistently. The affluent and the poor, people with homes and the homeless—while our problems are hugely different, in some ways we all struggle because we often feel unseen.

I firmly believe that when any of us feel stuck or that we don't have a chance, we are likely to think less about consequences and engage in things that would more likely be destructive to ourselves and others. And yet I also firmly believe that being seen and forging connections is the antidote.

What Danny experienced on the radio after being arrested is what I call a "Block moment"—an extraordinary turn of events that we can experience or create ourselves that casts us or our work into a limelight of profound exposure to our audience. We should always be looking to capture or create moments like this, and recognize them when they come to us.

Today, my brother is a better man, striving to create his art. Every time I talk to him I feel the depth of his humanity warm inside my chest, like a balm of milk and honey.

I sometimes ponder: How many Dannies—lost, unseen, unheard geniuses—are there in the world today?

THANK-YOUS AND INSPIRATION

My grandmother

The Katalyst, Kevin Carroll

Michael Thomas, a tireless friend with saintlike composure and quiet strength; Maryann Karinch, for being a literary agent with intense humanity; Glenn Yeffeth, for wanting to publish *The Iconist* and for his truly amazing publishing house; Claire Schulz, for her guidance, excellence, and true inspiration as editor; Miki Alexandra Caputo as an outstanding copyeditor who had my back and made me better; Sarah Avinger, for contributing to the book's cover; Leah Wilson, Adrienne Lang, Alicia Kania, and the entire team at BenBella Books; Dr. Steven Nakana; Rose Francis and Thandiwe Nakana for their joy, intelligence, and goodness; May Arden for her help and faith; and Mark Slotemaker for his inspired design.

Shaw Thomas, Mason Thomas, Hudson Thomas, Jelani Memory, Melanie Pullen, Holt McCallany, Julie Wilson, Paul Bronkar, Danette MacGregor, Emily Crumpacker, Marcus Swanson, David Rae, my father, Prof. Hector Vila of Middlebury College, Dr. Gareth M. Austin and the London School of Economics, Manhattanville College, Westchester Community College, Professors

Lawson Bowling and James Bryan of Manhattanville College, D'Wayne Edwards, Bob Proffitt, Mason and Candy Heydt, Clive Wilkinson, Dr. E. H. Hunt, Heather Metcalfe, Nathan "Natron" Andrews, Donwan Harrell, Jahayra Harrell, Manu, Scott Foster, Randall, David Bentley, Molly D'Amour, Michael Humphrey, Joanne Gordon, Cort Johnson, Bluegrass Biggs, Bibi McGill, John Elliott, Jeff Elliott, Chris Wojda, Tsilli Pines, Rowan Trollope, Malcolm Gladwell, Kramer Morgenthau, Anna and Elliott, Ayr Robinson Rein, and Hillary Harris.

REFERENCES AND IMAGE CREDITS

Chapter 2

Patrick Burgoyne, "São Paulo: The City That Said No to Advertising," *Bloomberg Businessweek*, June 18, 2007; www.businessweek.com/stories/2007-06-18/s-o-paulo-the-city-that-said-no-to-advertisingbusinessweek-business-news-stock-market-and-financial-advice, accessed December 26, 2014.

Paul Surgi Speck and Michael T. Elliott, "Predictors of Advertising Avoidance in Print and Broadcast Media," *Journal of Advertising* 26, no. 3 (Autumn, 1997): 61–76, www.jstor.org/stable/4189042.

Vincent Bevins, "São Paulo Advertising Goes Underground," *Financial Times*, September 6, 2010, www.ft.com/content/5ad26f14-b9e6-11df-8804-00144feabdco.

Rex A. Hudson, ed. *Brazil: A Country Study* (Washington, DC: GPO for the Library of Congress, 1997), countrystudies.us/brazil/.

New York City Global Partners, *Best Practice: Clean City Act*, April 2011, www1.nyc.gov/assets/globalpartners/downloads/pdf/Sao%20Paulo_CleanCityAct.pdf.

Cord Jefferson, "A Happy, Flourishing City with No Advertising." *Good*, December 25, 2011, www.good.is/articles/a-happy-flourishing-city-with-no-advertising.

Bob Garfield, "Clearing the Air," NPR, *On the Media*, www.onthemedia.org/story/129390-clearing-the-air/, April 20, 2007.

Chapter 3

Kristen Conway-Gomez et al., "Population and Natural Resources Conceptual Framework: How Does Population Growth Affect the Availability of Resources?," online module, ed. M. Solem et al., AAG Centre for Global Geography Education, globalgeography.aag.org/PopulationandNaturalResources1e/CF_PopNatRes_Jan10/CF_PopNatRes_Jan108.html, accessed February 17, 2015.

"Cutting Through Advertising Clutter," CBS News, September 17, 2006, www.cbsnews
.com/news/cutting-through-advertising-clutter/.

Louise Story, "Anywhere the Eye Can See, It's Likely to See an Ad," *New York Times*,
January 15, 2007, www.nytimes.com/2007/01/15/business/media/15everywhere
.html.

Oksana Tunikova, "How Many Ads Do You Actually See Daily?," StopAd, April 6, 2018,
www.stopad.io/blog/ads-seen-daily.

Ron Marshall, "How Many Ads Do You See in One Day?," September 10, 2015, www
.redcrowmarketing.com/2015/09/10/many-ads-see-one-day/.

Martin Hilbert and Priscila López, "The World's Technological Capacity to Store,
Communicate, and Compute Information," *Science* 332, no. 6025 (April 2011):
60–65, doi:10.1126/science.1200970.

Charles Arthur, "What's a Zettabyte? By 2015, the Internet Will Know, Says Cisco,"
Guardian, June 9, 2011, www.theguardian.com/technology/blog/2011/jun/29
/zettabyte-data-internet-cisco.

Todd Hoff, "How Big Is a Petabyte, Exabyte, Zettabyte, or a Yottabyte?," *High Scalability*
(blog), September 11, 2012, highscalability.com/blog/2012/9/11/how-big-is-a
-petabyte-exabyte-zettabyte-or-a-yottabyte.html.

Adrian F. Ward et al., "Brain Drain: The Mere Presence of One's Own Smartphone
Reduces Available Cognitive Capacity," *Journal of the Association for Consumer
Research* 2, no. 2 (April 2017): doi:10.1086/691462.

Robinson Meyer, "Your Smartphone Reduces Your Brainpower, Even If It's Just Sitting
There," *Atlantic*, August 2, 2017, www.theatlantic.com/technology/archive/2017/08
/a-sitting-phone-gathers-brain-dross/535476/.

Ruth Alexander, "Are Search Engine Results Accurate?," BBC News, February 20, 2012,
www.bbc.com/news/magazine-17068044.

Chapter 4

Linda Stone, "Just Breathe: Building the Case for Email Apnea," *Huffington Post*,
February 8, 2008, www.huffingtonpost.com/linda-stone/just-breathe-building-the
_b_85651.html.

"Three Technology Revolutions," Pew Research Center, www.pewinternet.org/three
-technology-revolutions/, accessed February 2014.

International Telecommunications Union Key Information and Communication
Technology Data, 2005–2017, www.itu.int/en/ITU-D/Statistics/Pages/facts/default
.aspx.

"Relatives Gather from Across the Country to Stare into Screens Together," *Onion*, December 25, 2013, www.theonion.com/articles/relatives-gather-from-across-the -country-to-stare,34842/.

Kirill Levchenko et al. "Click Trajectories: End-to-End Analysis of the Spam Value Chain," in *Proceedings of the 2011 IEEE Symposium on Security and Privacy, SP '11* (Washington, DC: IEEE Computer Society, 2011), doi:10.1109/SP.2011.24.

Paul Sawers, "Dropbox Opens Trading at $29, up 38% on IPO Price," *Venture Beat*, March 23, 2018, www.venturebeat.com/2018/03/23/dropbox-opens-trading-at-29 -up-38-on-ipo-price.

Chapter 5

Tim Goodman, "Tim Goodman's TV Review: FX's *Lights Out* Forgoes Boxing Cliches to Make for Compelling Drama," *Hollywood Reporter*, January 9, 2011, www .hollywoodreporter.com/review/tim-goodmans-tv-review-fxs-69748.

Holt McCallany, interview by Jamie Mustard. , December 13, 2018.

Maureen Ryan, "TV Peaks Again in 2016: Could It Hit 500 Shows in 2017?," *Variety*, December 21, 2016, https://variety.com/2016/tv/news/peak-tv-2016-scripted-tv -programs-1201944237/.

Ray Richmond, "TCA: FX's John Landgraf Not Discouraged by *Lights Out, Terriers* Ratings Woes," *Deadline Hollywood*, January 15, 2011, www.deadline.com/2011/01 /tca-fxs-john-landgraf-not-discouraged-by-lights-out-terriers-ratings-woes.

Sean O'Neal, "FX Cancels *Lights Out*," AV Club, March 24, 2011, www.avclub.com/article /fx-cancels-emlights-outem-53619.

Ann Friedman, "Overwhelmed and Creeped Out," *New Yorker*, February 26, 2013, www .newyorker.com/culture/culture-desk/overwhelmed-and-creeped-out.

Chapter 6

Jennifer Liberto, "The Unemployed Psyche: Job Searching for So Long Crushed My Soul," CNN Business, August 8, 2014, https://money.cnn.com/2014/08/05/news /economy/longterm-unemployed-depression/.

"Do Online Job Search Sites Work?," CNBC, January 27, 2011, www.cnbc.com/ id/41304850, accessed November 7, 2014.

Lauren Weber, "Your Résumé vs. Oblivion: Inundated Companies Resort to Software to Sift Job Applications for Right Skills," *Wall Street Journal*, January 24, 2012, http:// online.wsj.com/article/SB10001424052970204624204577178941034941330.html.

Kirsten Weir, "Alone in 'the Hole': Psychologists Probe the Mental Health Effects of Solitary Confinement," *Monitor on Psychology* 43, no. 5 (2012): www.apa.org /monitor/2012/05/solitary.

Chapter 7

"UFC's Chael Sonnen Hired by ESPN After Fox Firing," AP News, November 11, 2014, www.apnews.com/310882d7f0624335a8d821198af449c6.

"Is Chael Sonnen MMA's Muhammad Ali?," Fox Sports, December 17, 2011, www .foxsports.com/ufc/story/is-chael-sonnen-mma-muhammad-ali-121711.

Chapter 8

"What to Do When There Are Too Many Product Choices on Store Shelves?" *Consumer Reports*, March 2014. www.consumerreports.org/cro/magazine/2014/03/too-many -product-choices-in-supermarkets/index.htm.

Barry Schwartz, "The Paradox of Choice," TEDGlobal Talk, July 2005, www.ted.com /talks/barry_schwartz_on_the_paradox_of_choice?language=en.

Malcolm Gladwell, *Blink: The Power of Thinking Without Thinking* (New York: Little, Brown, 2005), 142–43; see reference to Sheena S. Iyengar and Mark R. Lepper on page 69.

"When Choice Is Demotivating: Can One Desire Too Much of a Good Thing?," *Journal of Personality and Social Psychology* 79, no. 6 (2000): 995–1006.

Alina Tugend, "Too Many Choices: A Problem That Can Paralyze," *New York Times*, February 26, 2010, www.nytimes.com/2010/02/27/your-money/27shortcuts.html.

George Loewenstein, Daniel Read, and Roy F. Baumeister, eds., *Time and Decision: Economic and Psychological Perspectives on Intertemporal Choice* (New York: Russell Sage, 2003).

John Tierney, "Do You Suffer from Decision Fatigue?," *New York Times*, August 17, 2011, www.nytimes.com/2011/08/21/magazine/do-you-suffer-from-decision-fatigue.html.

Chapter 9

John Locke, *The Works of John Locke*, vol. 9 (London: W. Otridge and Son, 1812).

Haig Kouyoumdjian, "Learning Through Visuals: Visual Imagery in the Classroom," *Psychology Today*, July 20, 2012, www.psychologytoday.com/us/blog/get-psyched /201207/learning-through-visuals.

K. L. Alesandrini, "Pictures and Adult Learning," *Instructional Science* 13, no. 1 (May 1984): 63–77, https://link.springer.com/article/10.1007/BF00051841.

Shark Tank. episode 7.13, aired January 8, 2016, on ABC, https://vimeo.com/151256962.

Chapter 10

Mario Livio, *The Equation That Couldn't Be Solved: How Mathematical Genius Discovered the Language of Symmetry* (New York: Simon & Schuster, 2005), 233.

Joanna E. Scheib, Steven W. Gangestad, and Randy Thornhill, "Facial Attractiveness, Symmetry, and Cues to Good Genes," *Proceedings of the Royal Society B* 266, no. 1431 (September 1999): 1913–17, doi:10.1098/rspb.1999.0866.

David I. Perrett et al., "Symmetry and Human Facial Attractiveness," *Evolution and Human Behavior* 20, no. 5 (June 1999): 295–307, doi:10.1016/S1090-5138(99)00014-8.

Chapter 11

Vincent Scully, "Louis I. Kahn and the Ruins of Rome," *Engineering & Science* 56, no. 2 (Winter 1993): 3–13, http://calteches.library.caltech.edu/621/2/Scully.pdf.

Christopher Hawthorne, "Louis Kahn: Bad Dad, Great Architect," *Slate*, November 14, 2003. www.slate.com/articles/arts/culturebox/2003/11/hop_on_pop.html.

Inga Saffron, "Obituary: Anne Tyng, 91, Groundbreaking Architect," *Philadelphia Inquirer*, January 7, 2012, http://articles.philly.com/2012-01-07/news/30602107_1_anne-tyng-louis-i-kahn-architecture-school, accessed February 9, 2015.

Jayne Clark, "USA Today and Good Morning America's 7 New Wonders of the World," *USA Today*, December 22, 2006, http://usatoday30.usatoday.com/travel/news/2006-11-23-7-wonders-grand-canyon_x.htm.

Clive Wilkinson, interview by Jamie Mustard, October 12, 2018.

Chapter 12

"High Fashion Crime Scenes" (exhibition page), Wirtz Art, www.wirtzart.com/exhibition/high-fashion-crime-scenes/, accessed April 10, 2019.

Melanie Pullen, *Violent Times* (still-photography series, 2005–2009), www.melaniepullen.com/matter/.

Kramer Morgenthau, interview by Jamie Mustard, October 15, 2018.

Chapter 13

Philip Hale on Beethoven's Ninth Symphony in the *Musical Record*, Boston, June 1, 1899.

Ferdinand Praeger, "On the Fallacy of the Repetition of Parts in the Classical Form," *Proceedings of the Royal Musical Association* 9 (1882), 2.

Estelle Caswell, "Why We Really, Really, Really Like Repetition in Music," Vox, October 13, 2017, www.vox.com/videos/2017/10/13/16469744/repetition-in-music.

Cam Lindsay, "The Dandy Warhols' Courtney Taylor-Taylor Passionately Ranks the Band's LPs," *Vice*, January 24, 2019, www.vice.com/en_us/article/3kgzmk/rank-your-records-the-dandy-warhols-courtney-taylor-taylor.

Kory Grow, "Rage Against the Machine Look Back on 20 Years of 'Killing in the Name,'" *Spin*, November 19, 2012, www.spin.com/articles/rage-against-the-machine-killing-in-the-name-anniversary-interview/.

"Quincy Jones on Battling Michael Jackson, Befriending Sinatra," CBC News: The National, September 17, 2018, www.youtube.com/watch?v=EK6M5jPsolQ.

Ian K. Smith, "Top 20 Political Songs," *New Statesman*, March 25, 2010, http://www.newstatesman.com/music/2010/03/top-20-political-songs, accessed January 8, 2015.

Adam Grant, "The Surprising Habits of Original Thinkers," TED Talk, April 26, 2016, https://www.youtube.com/watch?v=fxbCHn6gE3U.

Chapter 14

Martin Luther King Jr., "I Have a Dream," August 28, 1963, transcript, National Archives and Records Administration, www.archives.gov/press/exhibits/dream-speech.pdf.

Mark Donnelly, *Britain in the Second World War* (New York: Routledge, 1999), 15.

"To Be More Persuasive, Repeat Yourself," Association for Psychological Science, April 20, 2016, www.psychologicalscience.org/news/minds-business/to-be-more-persuasive-repeat-yourself.html.

Stefan Schulz-Hardt, Annika Giersiepen, and Andreas Mojzisch (2016), Preference-Consistent Information Repetitions During Discussion: Do They Affect Subsequent Judgments and Decisions?," *Journal of Experimental Social Psychology* 64 (January 2016): doi:10.1016/j.jesp.2016.01.009.

Chapter 16

D'Wayne Edwards, interview by Chris Young, January 2014.

Gary Warnett, "How Run-DMC Earned Their Adidas Stripes," MR PORTER, May 2016, www.mrporter.com/daily/how-run-dmc-earned-their-adidas-stripes/939.

Erik Parker, "Hip-Hop Goes Commercial," *Village Voice*, September 10, 2002, www.villagevoice.com/2002-09-10/news/hip-hop-goes-commercial/.

"About Us," Wall Drug, http://www.walldrug.com/about-us.

D'Wayne Edwards, interview by Jamie Mustard, August 22, 2018.

Chapter 17

Eugene F. Provenzo Jr., "Friedrich Froebel's Gifts: Connecting the Spiritual and Aesthetic to the Real World of Play and Learning," *American Journal of Play* 2, no. 1 (Summer 2009): www.journalofplay.org/sites/www.journalofplay.org/files/pdf -articles/2-1-article-friedrich-froebels-gifts.pdf.

Emily Deruy, "How to Predict a Baby's First Word," *Atlantic*, December 9, 2016, www .theatlantic.com/education/archive/2016/12/how-to-predict-a-babys-first-word /510146/.

Mike Rowe, "Several Months Ago, I Took Umbrage," Facebook, September 19, 2017, https://www.facebook.com/TheRealMikeRowe/.

Travis Andrews, "Nordstrom Is Selling Jeans Caked in Fake Dirt for Hundreds of Dollars," *Washington Post*, August 26, 2017, www.washingtonpost.com/news /morning-mix/wp/2017/04/26/nordstrom-is-selling-jeans-caked-in-fake-dirt-for -hundreds-of-dollars/.

Chapter 18

Al Ries, "Long Slogans Are Absolutely, Positively More Effective than Short Ones," *Ad Age*, September 7, 2010, https://adage.com/article/al-ries/long-slogans-absolutely -positively-effective-short/145755/.

Chapter 20

Sergio Zyman, *The End of Marketing as We Know It*, 1st ed. (New York: HarperBusiness, 1999), 230.

Al Ries and Laura Ries, *The Fall of Advertising and the Rise of PR* (New York: HarperCollins, 2002).

Kevin J. Clancy and Randy L. Stone, "Don't Blame the Metrics," *Harvard Business Review*, June 2005, https://hbr.org/2005/06/dont-blame-the-metrics.

Larry Alton, "How Corporate Distrust Is Reshaping Advertising," *Adweek*, August 17, 2017, www.adweek.com/digital/larry-alton-guest-post-how-corporate-distrust-is -reshaping-advertising/.

Phil Styrlund and Tom Hayes, *Relevance: Matter More*, ed. Marian Deegan (n.p.: Mary Mae and Sons, 2014).

Crazy People, directed by Tony Bill (1990; Paramount Pictures, 2004), DVD.

Chapter 21

Kate Freeman, "98% of Americans Distrust the Internet," Mashable, July 19, 2012, http://
mashable.com/2012/07/19/americans-distrust-the-internet/.

Gallup News Service, *Gallup Poll Social Series: Governance*, September, 2010, https://
news.gallup.com/poll/143273/trust-mass-media-pdf.aspx.

Lymari Maralis, "U.S. Distrust in Media Hits New High," Gallup, September 21, 2012,
http://www.gallup.com/poll/157589/distrust-media-hits-new-high.aspx, accessed
February 12, 2015.

GfK Roper Public Affairs & Corporate Communications, *AP-National Constitution Center
Poll*, August 2012, http://surveys.ap.org/data/GfK/AP-NCC%20Poll%20August%20
GfK%202012%20Topline%20FINAL_1st%20release.pdf.

Anna-Louise Jackson, Anthony Feld, and Melinda Grenier, "Domino's Brutally Honest
Ads Offset Slow Consumer Spending," *Bloomberg Businessweek*, October 17, 2011,
www.bloomberg.com/news/articles/2011-10-17/domino-s-brutally-honest-ads
-offset-slowing-consumer-spending.

Adrian Campos, "Why Domino's Spent Millions to Fix Its Pizza," The Motley Fool,
November 20, 2013, www.fool.com/investing/general/2013/11/20/why-dominos
-spent-millions-to-fix-its-pizza.aspx.

Chapter 22

Ken Doctor, "The Newsonomics of the Millennial Moment," Nieman, October 8, 2014,
www.niemanlab.org/2014/10/the-newsonomics-of-the-millennial-moment/.

Marc Gurman, "A Look at 'the Average' iTunes Library," 9to5Mac, January 4, 2011,
http://9to5mac.com/2011/01/04/a-look-at-the-average-itunes-library/.

Kristen Purcell, Joanna Brenner, and Lee Rainie, "Search Engine Use 2012, " Pew Research
Center's Internet & American Life Project, March 9, 2012, http://www.pewinternet
.org/2012/03/09/search-engine-use-2012/, accessed February 12, 2012.

Afterword

Chris Martins, "In Their Right Place: Ranking 10 Radiohead 'Creep' Covers," *Spin*,
September 22, 2012, www.spin.com/2012/09/radiohead-creep-covers-ranked
-weezer-kelly-clarkson-korn.

John M. Bolland, "Hopelessness and Risk Behaviour Among Adolescents Living in
High-Poverty Inner-City Neighbourhoods," *Journal of Adolescence* 26, no. 2 (2003):
145–58.

Barry Schwartz, "The Paradox of Choice," TEDGlobal Talk, July 2005, TED.com, www .ted.com/talks/barry_schwartz_on_the_paradox_of_choice?language=en.

Sarah A. Stoddard et al., "Social Connections, Trajectories of Hopelessness, and Serious Violence in Impoverished Urban Youth," *Journal of Youth and Adolescence* 40, no. 3 (March 2011): 278–95, www.ncbi.nlm.nih.gov/pmc/articles/PMC3105375/.

Carol Graham and Sergio Pinto, "Unhappiness in America: Desperation in White Towns, Resilience and Diversity in the Cities," Brookings, September 29, 2016, www.brookings.edu/research/unhappiness-in-america-desperation-in-white-towns -resilience-and-diversity-in-the-cities/.

Image Credits

Images from *The Combat Soldiers* (pages 112–117) by Melanie Pullen, reprinted with permission from Melanie Pullen.

Wall Drug sign at the Taj Mahal (page 164) from the Hustead Family Archive, reprinted with permission from Rick Hustead.

Sports Ball Artifacts (page 169) by Swanson Studio, reprinted with permission from Kevin Carroll.

Author photo by Connor Meyer.

All other art by Mark Slotemaker.

INDEX

ABOUT THE AUTHOR

JAMIE MUSTARD is an expert on STANDING OUT and making something endure. He is a leading authority on brand, art, design, and media perception in the physical world and the economics of attention. Steeped in the worlds of technology, product engagement, and the creative arts, Jamie consults with leading companies, CEOs, creative artists, public servants, entrepreneurs, and thought leaders, getting their messages, products, brands, and ideas to STAND OUT to their desired audiences.

An avid consumer of popular culture and a graduate of the London School of Economics with a degree in economics and economic history, Jamie has almost two decades of experience in technological and industrial public relations both nationally and abroad. He has expertise in strategic messaging, demand generation, product development, creative production, and story and branding, and has consulted for Intel, Cisco, Symantec, and Adidas, to name but a few. As a creative artist, Jamie has worked in music, fine art, and documentary film production. His work has screened at the Lincoln Center in New York City, and Kevin Turan of the *Los Angeles Times* called the film he produced, *Showbiz Is My Life*, "beguiling." He is currently working on a large-format art exhibition and an experimental opera album—both using his signature, the primal laws of Blocks.